Displays spanning 400 million years recount the City's fascinating history. Nowhere else could you find the famous Tay Whale, the world's oldest Astrolabe and a Rossetti masterpiece all under one roof.

2

—

3

First published in 2018 by Big Sky Books.

Big Sky Books
Drumderfit
North Kessock
by Inverness
www.bigsky.scot

Picture by Alan Richardson
Words by Anna Day
Design by Andrew Forteath
Printed by Bell and Bain, Glasgow.

ISBN 978-0956957870

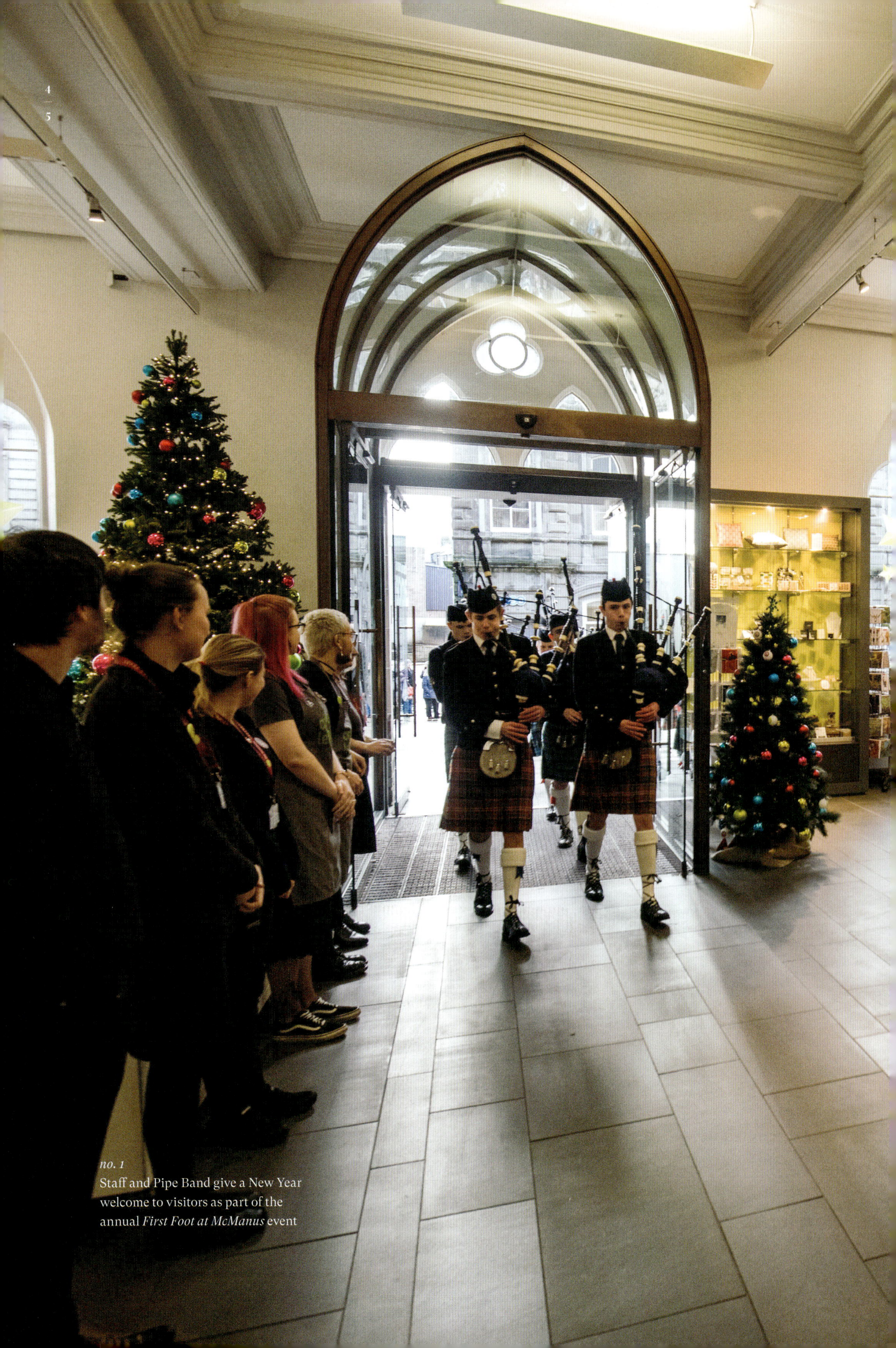

no. 1
Staff and Pipe Band give a New Year welcome to visitors as part of the annual *First Foot at McManus* event

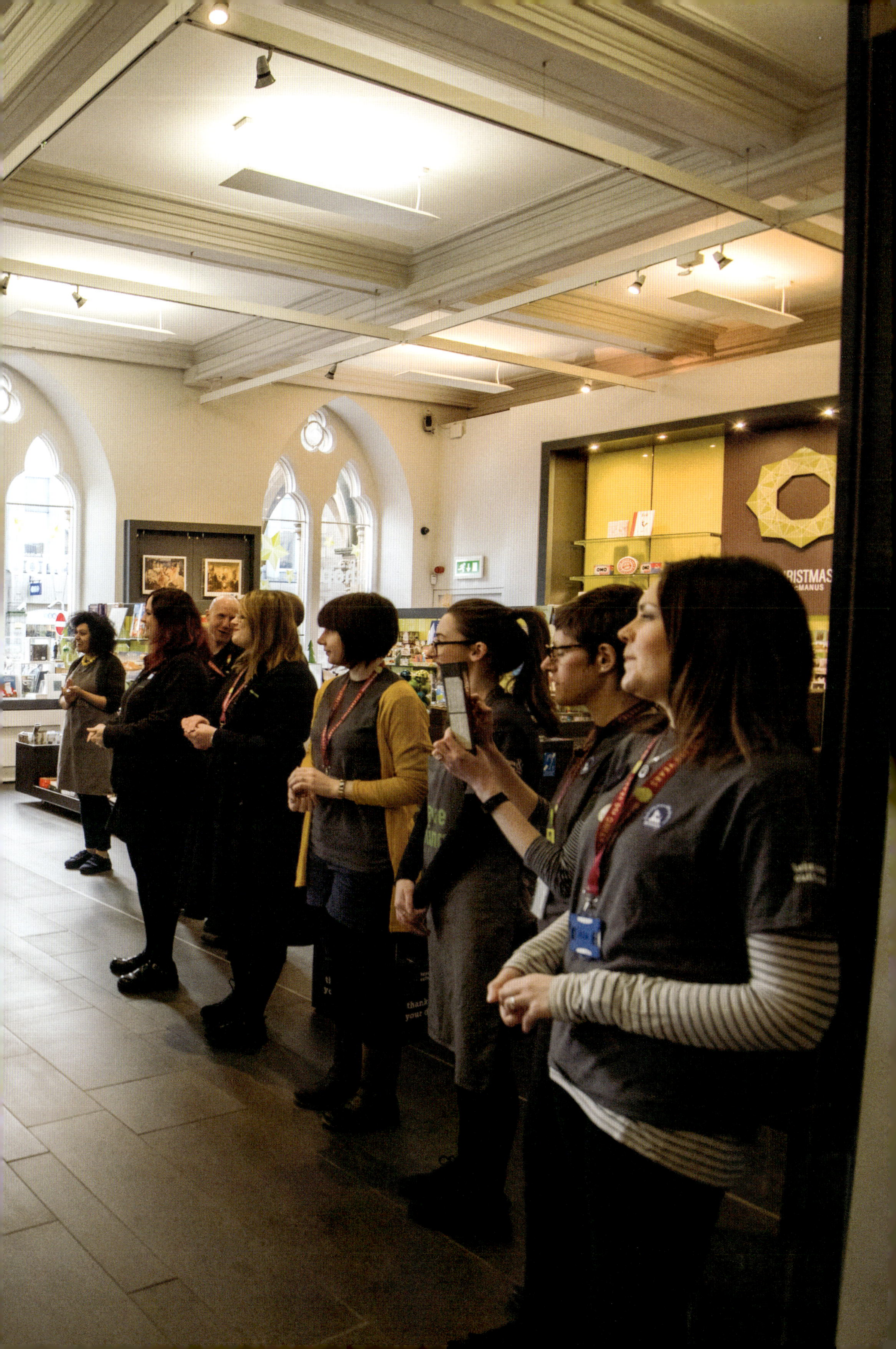
RISTMAS
MANUS

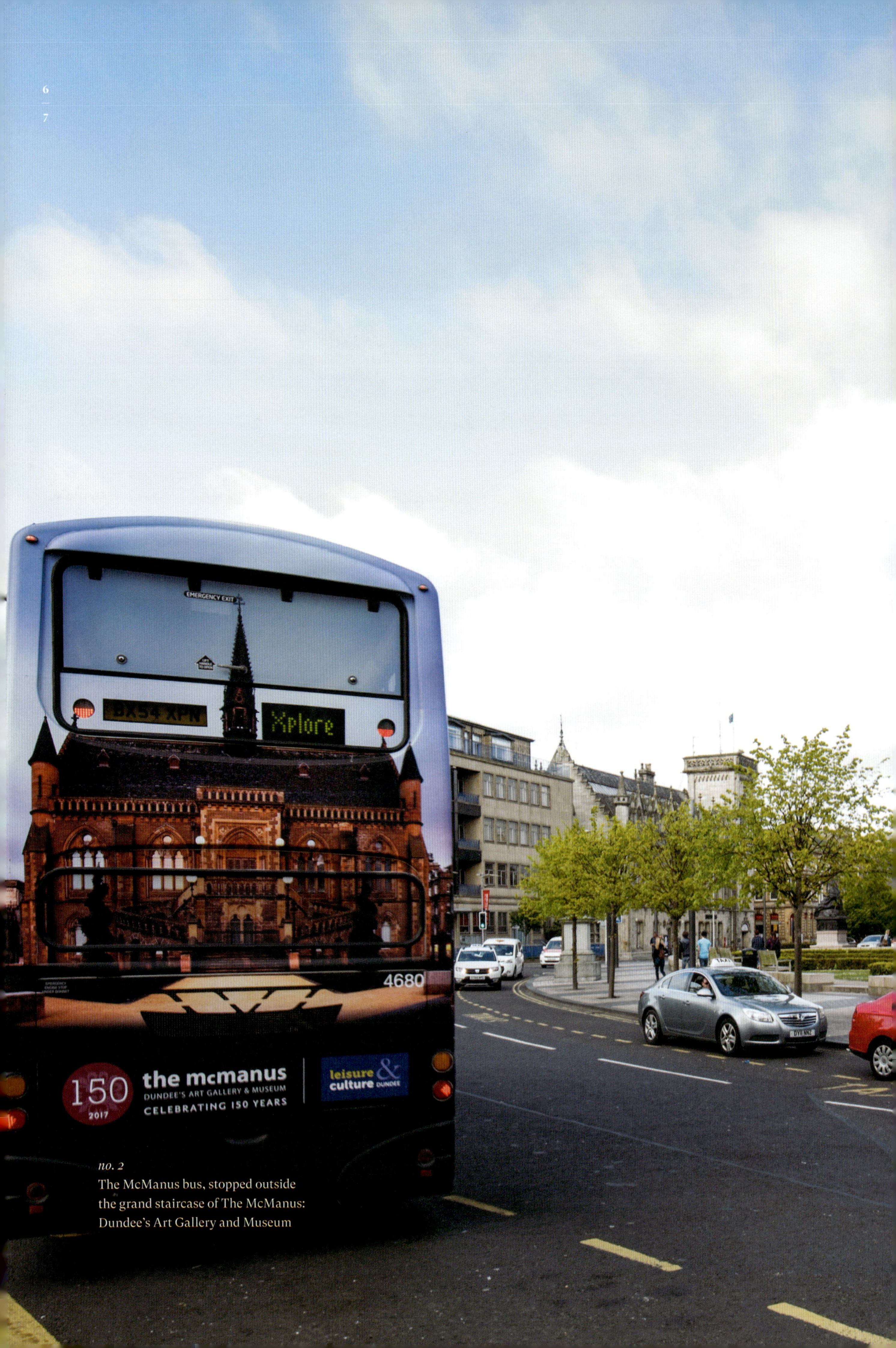

no. 2
The McManus bus, stopped outside the grand staircase of The McManus: Dundee's Art Gallery and Museum

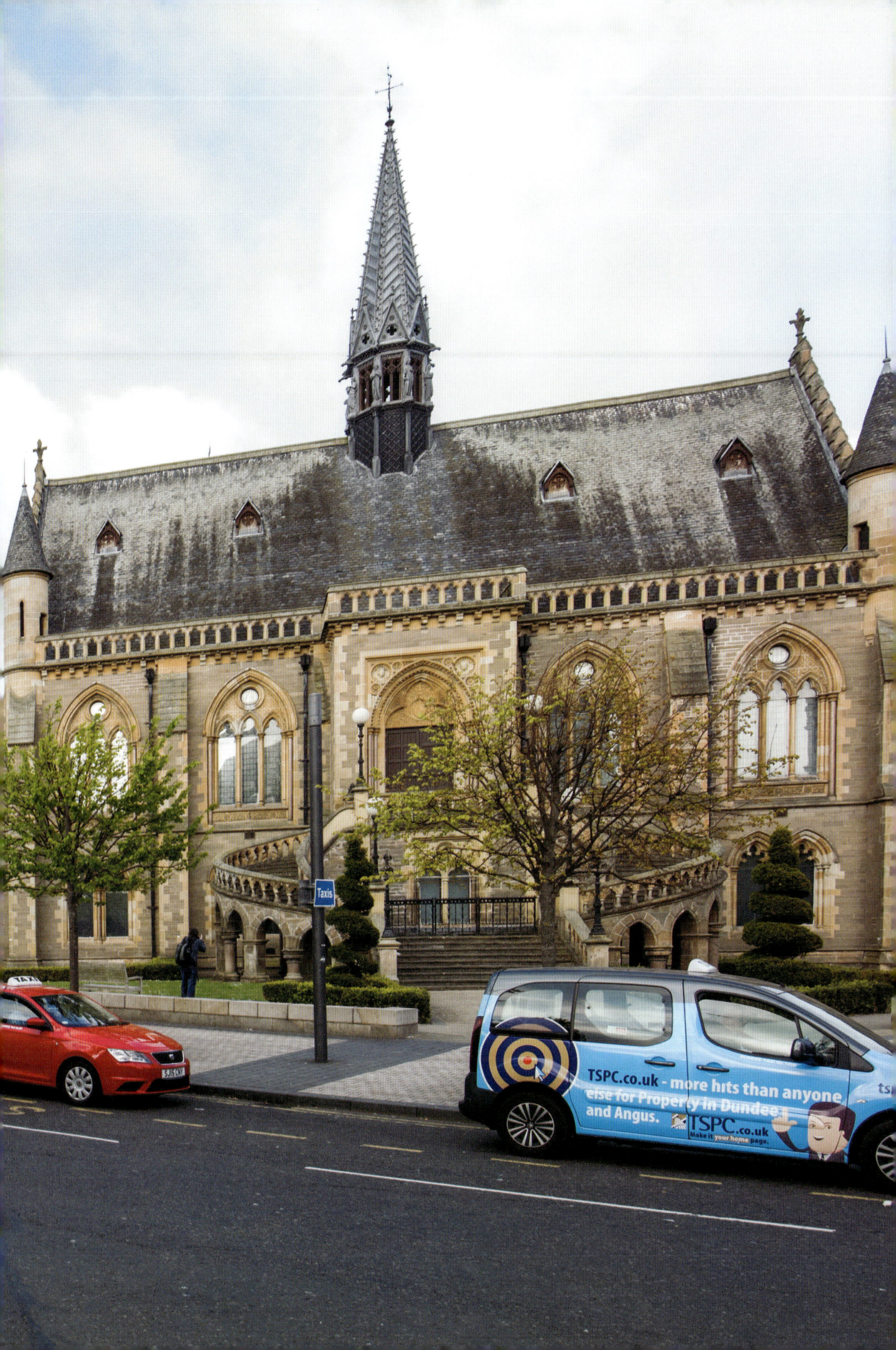
Taxis
TSPC.co.uk - more hits than anyone else for Property in Dundee and Angus.
TSPC.co.uk
Make it your home page.

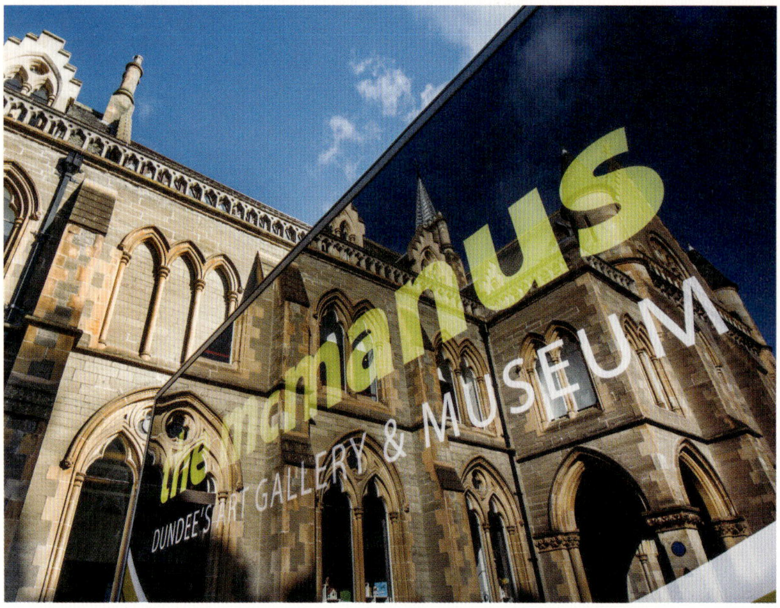

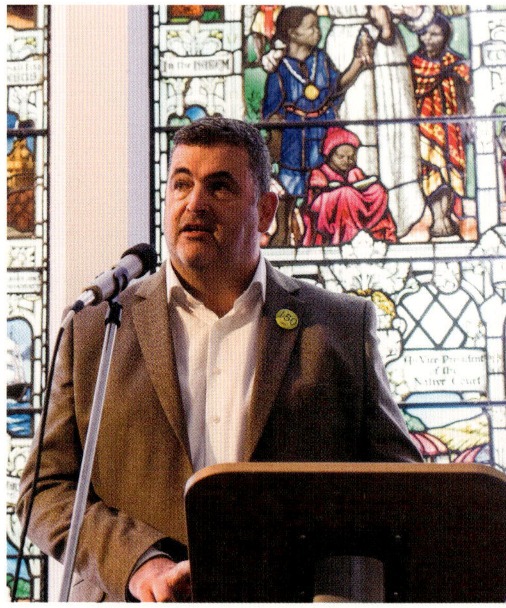

'In these pages you'll discover the story of a remarkable year for the museum where we engaged with more than 150,000 visitors.'

Introduction

In recent years, The McManus has developed exhibitions from our collections and worked with partners including the British Museum, V&A, National Museum of Scotland, Royal Collection, National Galleries of Scotland, Historic Environment Scotland.

I've had the privilege of overseeing the celebratory year of the 150th anniversary of the The McManus: Dundee's Art Gallery and Museum and what a year it has been. During the twelve months, we told the story of its exceptional collections through its exhibition and events programme.

We introduced The Maritime Quarter, a new permanent display of ship models highlighting Dundee's rich maritime history...

By creating this focus, our audiences got an insight into the collections and how we care for them. Artists and musicians were commissioned to respond to the collections, making new works in photography, film and soundscapes which as a legacy, have entered our collections.

To celebrate The McManus landmark 150th year in 2017, an exciting year-long programme was launched to engage, enrich and encourage creative participation in cultural activities.

In recent years, The McManus has developed exhibitions from our collections and worked with partners including the British Museum, V&A and the National Museum of Scotland to name a few. Collaborations with the institutions have been beneficial and has seen us share learning and deliver some excellent exhibitions through these partnerships.

However, we always considered 2017 as an opportunity to focus on and invite responses to our own collections. Following discussion, with our various stakeholders, we agreed to put our collection 'front and centre'. We wanted to tell stories about the collection, the people involved and about the magnificent George Gilbert Scott building.

Our highlights included the *Fire and Stone* exhibition which explored the local history and archaeology and the process behind creating contemporary responses to ancient metal and stone artefacts. Two stunning exhibitions *Out Of The Frame: Scottish Abstraction* and *Sense of Place* allowed visitors could revel in artworks by Wilhelmina Barns-Graham, Calum Innes and a major new acquisition by Victoria Morton. This included collection artworks by the Glasgow Boys, James McIntosh Patrick and Joan Eardley.

We introduced a new permanent display, *The Maritime Quarter*, an exciting new permanent display of ship models highlighting Dundee's rich maritime history, which also features some of the recently acquired DP&L models.

A project that has reached out across the city is *McManus 150: The People's Story*. It connected more than 9,000 people with the museum and collections. The People's Story was developed as part of a year-long programme of cultural activity delivered through a series of creative learning collaborations with partners, cultural agencies, individuals, community groups and networks across the city. Told through art, dance, music, theatre, film, and written and spoken word, it explored and documented the relationship between museum, the city's collections and Dundee's diverse communities. It opened with a first foot event to welcome our audiences back to The McManus for the new year and its highlight event in May 2017 was inspired by The McManus' past, present and future generations of visitors and supporters. Our two resident choirs were fantastic contributors throughout the year.

The *Dundee Preserves: Caring for the City's Collections* exhibition provided a rare opportunity to view some of the behind the scenes work carried out by conservation staff, and the chance to find out how new technology has helped us research our Egyptian Mummy, and take a look at paintings before and after conservation. Specially created work by artist Calum Colvin entitled *Museography: Calum Colvin Reflects on The McManus Collections*, drew inspiration from our collection and featuring Michael Marra, Robert Burns and William McGonagall amongst others. The 150th anniversary year culminated in two specially commissioned artworks created by leading Scottish artist Duncan Marquiss and musician Jonnie Common. Both were given special access to The McManus collections to create a large-scale video installation that was projected on the exterior of the building and a live music performance called *Drawn to Light*. This has been another significant year for loans, with work travelling to France, Spain, Japan and to various UK destinations. This year, our supporters group McManus 168 secured Heritage Lottery funding for a ground-breaking community project on the original subscribers to the building, which was funded entirely through public subscription. The staff and volunteers complete The McManus story. They show a level of dedication and commitment to their roles that allows us to function at the highest level, working together to tell the tale of the building and the collections.

The McManus is a dynamic museum fit for the 21st Century and another 150 years to follow. In these pages you'll discover the story of a remarkable year for the museum where we engaged with more than 150,000 visitors. The celebrations, collections and community work is detailed here in pictures by Alan Richardson. The thousands who love this museum are represented by a selection of our biggest fans – people who work, volunteer and visit here, in many different guises. They were asked to pick their favourite object and explain their relationship with the museum.

Billy Gartley, Head of Cultural Services.
Leisure & Culture Dundee.

The 150th anniversary year culminated in two specially commissioned artworks created by leading Scottish artist Duncan Marquiss and musician Jonnie Common.

The staff and volunteers complete The McManus story. They show a level of dedication and commitment to their roles that allows us to function at the highest level, working together to tell the tale of the building and the collections.

The McManus is a dynamic museum fit for the 21st Century and another 150 years to follow.

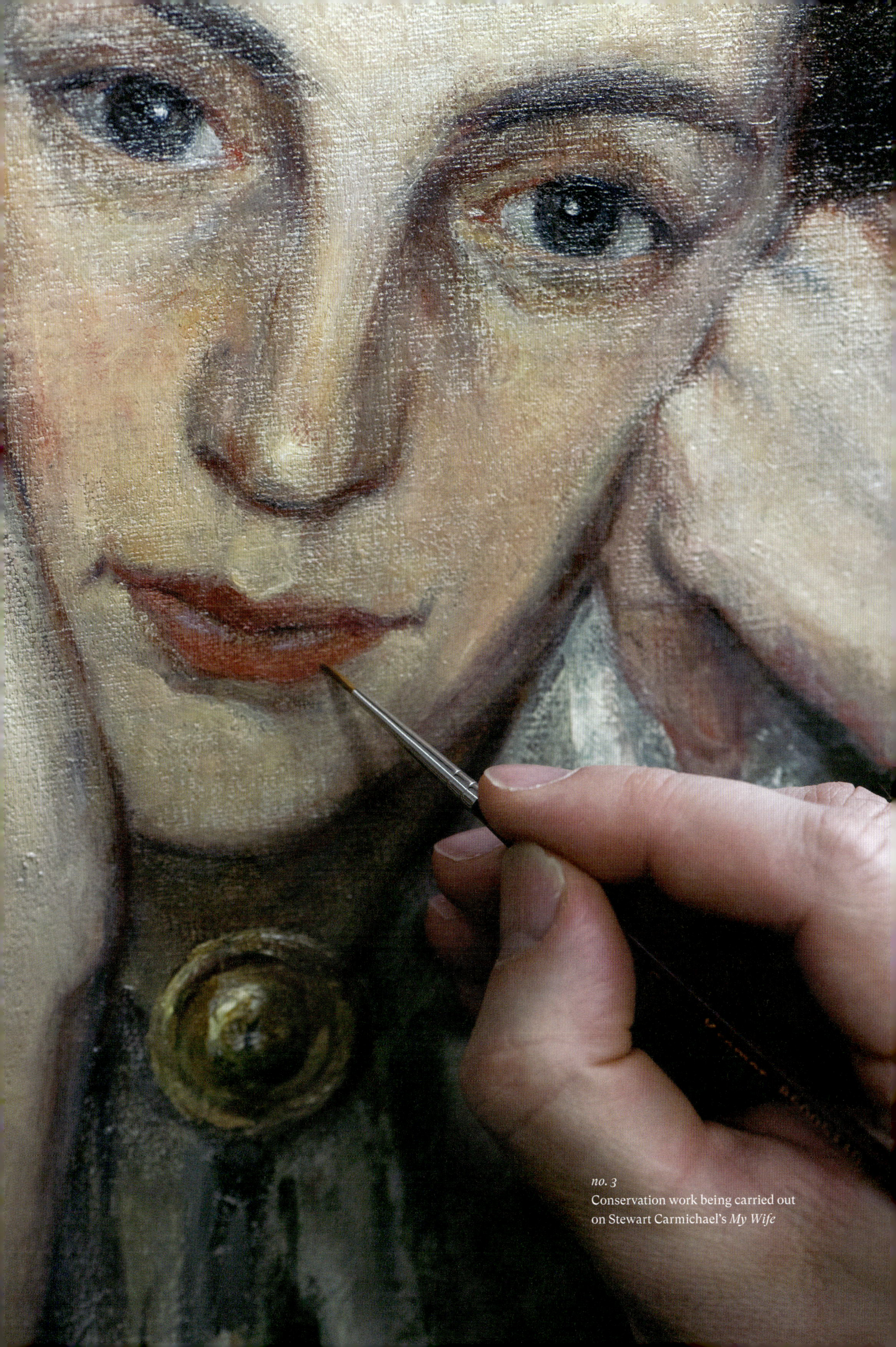

no. 3
Conservation work being carried out on Stewart Carmichael's *My Wife*

A Celel

oration

A Celebration

The sense of celebration, commemorating the 150th anniversary of The McManus was palpable from the opening day of the year, when pipers and staff greeted *first footing* Dundonians with warm words, hot drinks and a range of activities.

Throughout the following 365 days, the whole team was involved. Members of the front of house team, curators and management, all collaborated to show off the collections to the world. Certainly nobody in Dundee could miss out – from the bus that was adorned in images from the museum, to the specially brewed beer and the Christmas tree baubles, there was an element of the celebration that appealed to everybody.

The stars of the show, of course, were the objects and the stories they tell. In the Anniversary year, it was important to tell those stories in a new way. In *Museography: Calum Colvin Reflects on The McManus Collections*, Calum Colvin's works were installed throughout the museum as interventions into permanent displays. Colvin's multi-layered approach to image creation and storytelling provided visitors with a new context in which to view The McManus displays.

The exhibition opened in July. Calum said, "It felt in a sense that my whole career had been building up to the Museography project at McManus, that the nature of my work was going to fit the museum space in a highly appropriate way. The idea grew from a conversation with Billy Gartley, who suggested that placing my large photographic work within the galleries would resonate with the existing narrative structure of the displays and would underline the sense of history that the Collection epitomises. We quickly saw that a series of strategically placed 'interventions' of artworks within the permanent collection of paintings, artefacts and objects on display throughout the McManus would offer a kind of collection within the collection, and the objects within the photographs would complement the objects on display in a playful way. We also realised the subject of the works could equally resonate.

"In the end, the works we selected were inspired by my time at Dundee in a multitude of ways, and I hope they offered a fresh look at the McManus collections, so they had come full circle in a sense."

The year was punctuated by a celebratory 150th Anniversary day, echoing an event first held on 12th September 1867. The museum welcomed hosts of children, dignitaries and fans of the McManus in the doors, with pipers, singing and a very big cake. Every celebratory year needs a moment to pause and consider the past, present and future – the speeches, the people and the air of anticipation did just that.

The grand finale was an ambitious project, a commission of new and innovative work by some of the most exciting artists connected to Dundee, a light projection mapping event with brand new music composed for the event.

Drawn to Light was produced by Sion Parkinson. He said, "I immediately knew who I wanted to work with. Duncan Marquiss graduated from the University of Dundee's Duncan of Jordanstone College of Art and Design and had a solo exhibition at Dundee Contemporary Arts, so his Dundee connections were strong. Johnnie Common is from Dundee and has been making experimental music, so the fit seemed ideal.

"Initially, I had to foster a relationship with the McManus curatorial team who took the artists under their wing and provided access to the archives. Duncan brought together a strange, eclectic group of objects that formed a memory belonging to the museum. He filmed the items on a black turntable, so when they were spinning, it was almost as if you were looking at the museum's brain. It felt abstract but there is a link between these objects; what a museum can do is retain obscure and different things and hold them all at once.

Johnnie recorded the resonant frequency of every space, every gallery, every room, within the museum and then augmented and manipulated each sound so it became a musical tone. Then he composed with it, so his four songs were entirely recorded within the museum so again the museum is speaking or singing for itself. "Both artists came together in a music and light projection that was very special. There's a legacy to the event as well, an album of the music that Johnnie recorded and a film of the work that Duncan made."

Those works will become part of the collection of the museum, renewing and adding to the collection in a truly special act of celebration.

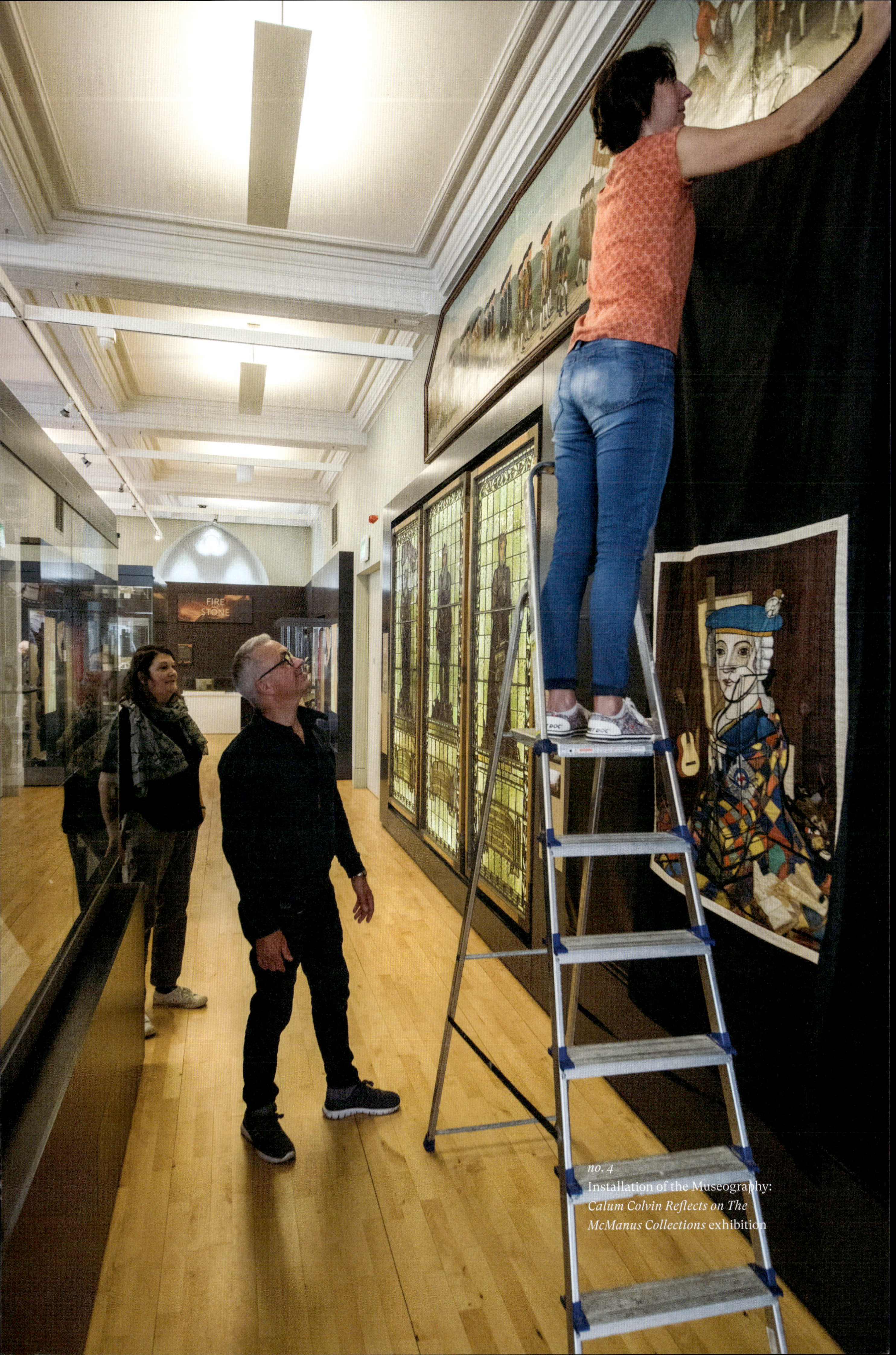

no. 4
Installation of the Museography: *Calum Colvin Reflects on The McManus Collections* exhibition

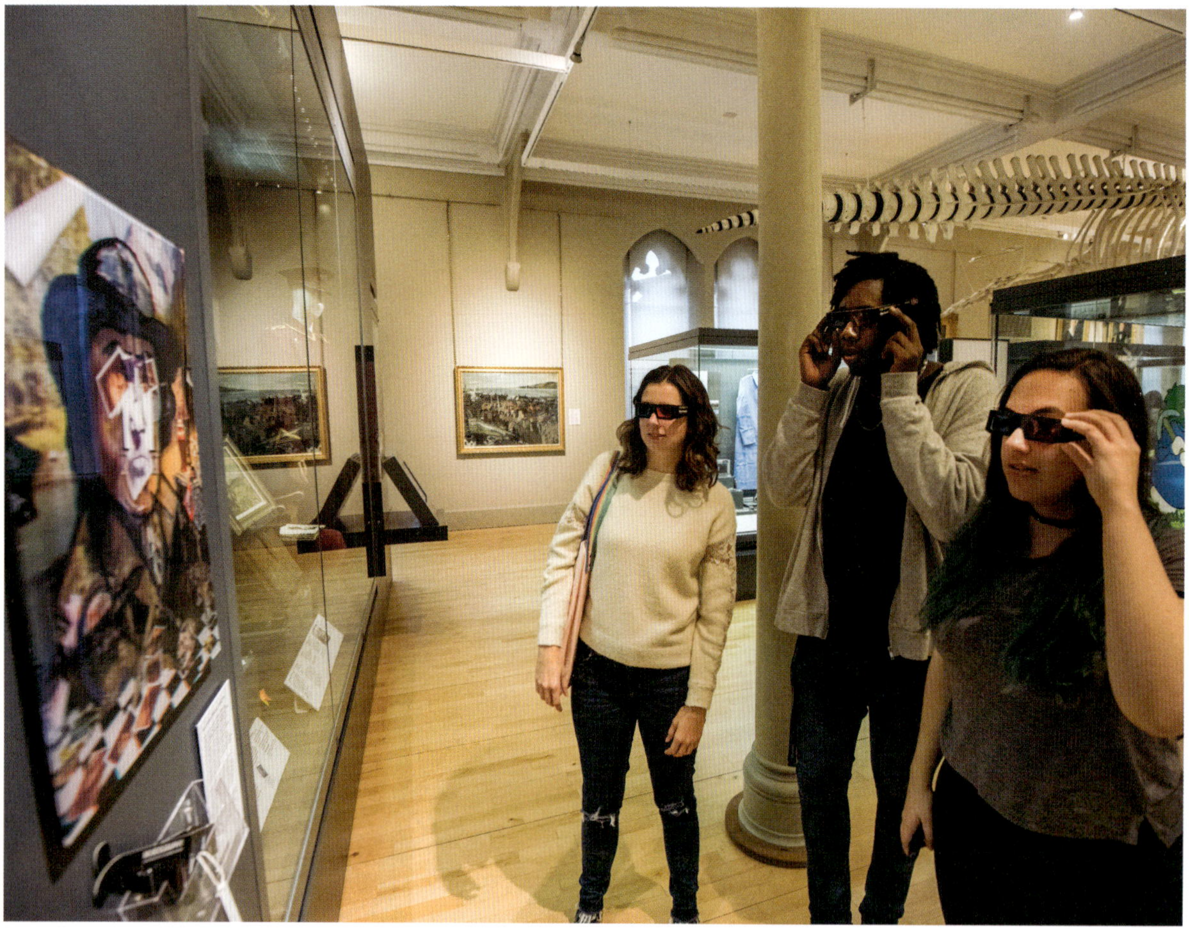

no. 5
Visitors view the 3D anaglyph of Calum Colvin's McGonagall artwork through 3D glasses

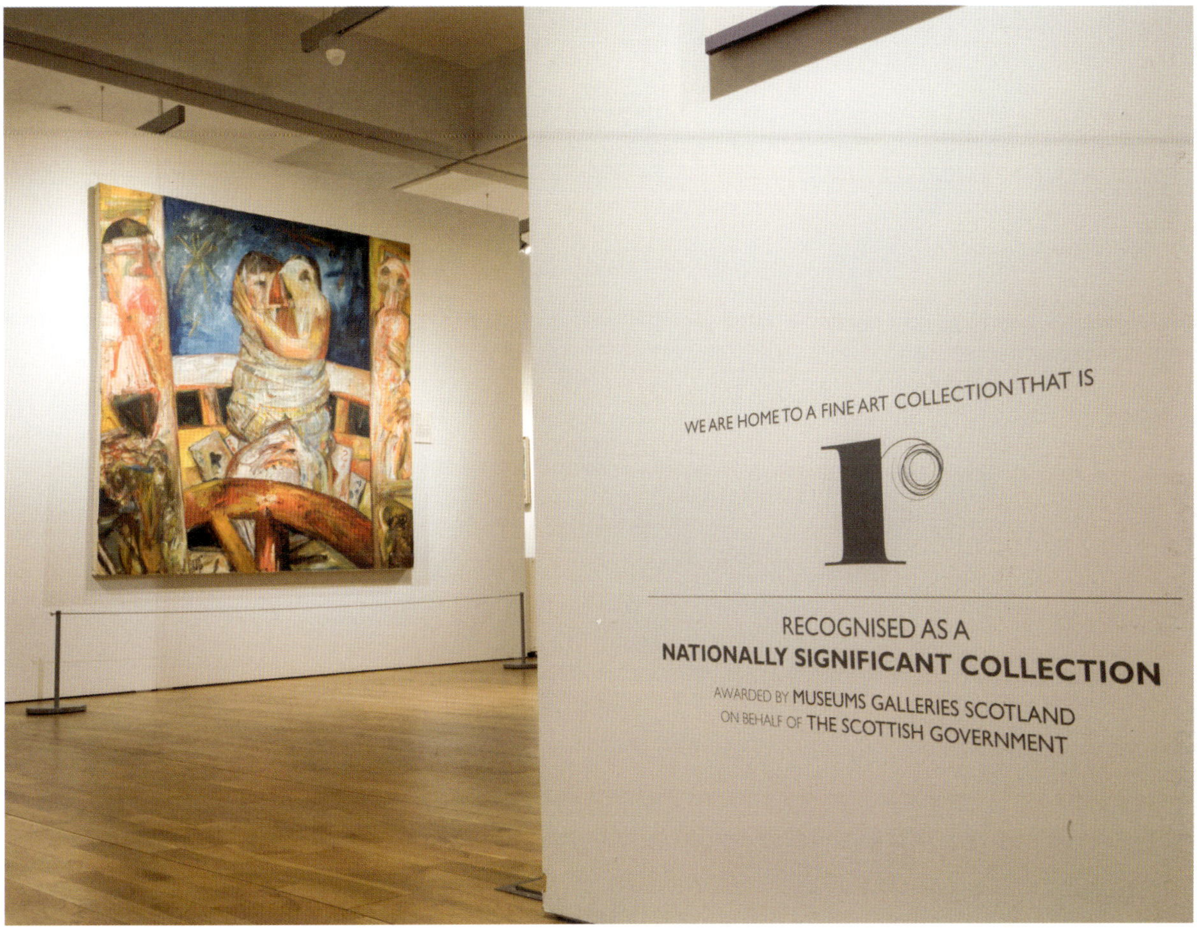

no. 6
The City's fine art in the *Sense of Place* exhibition is part of our three recognised collections

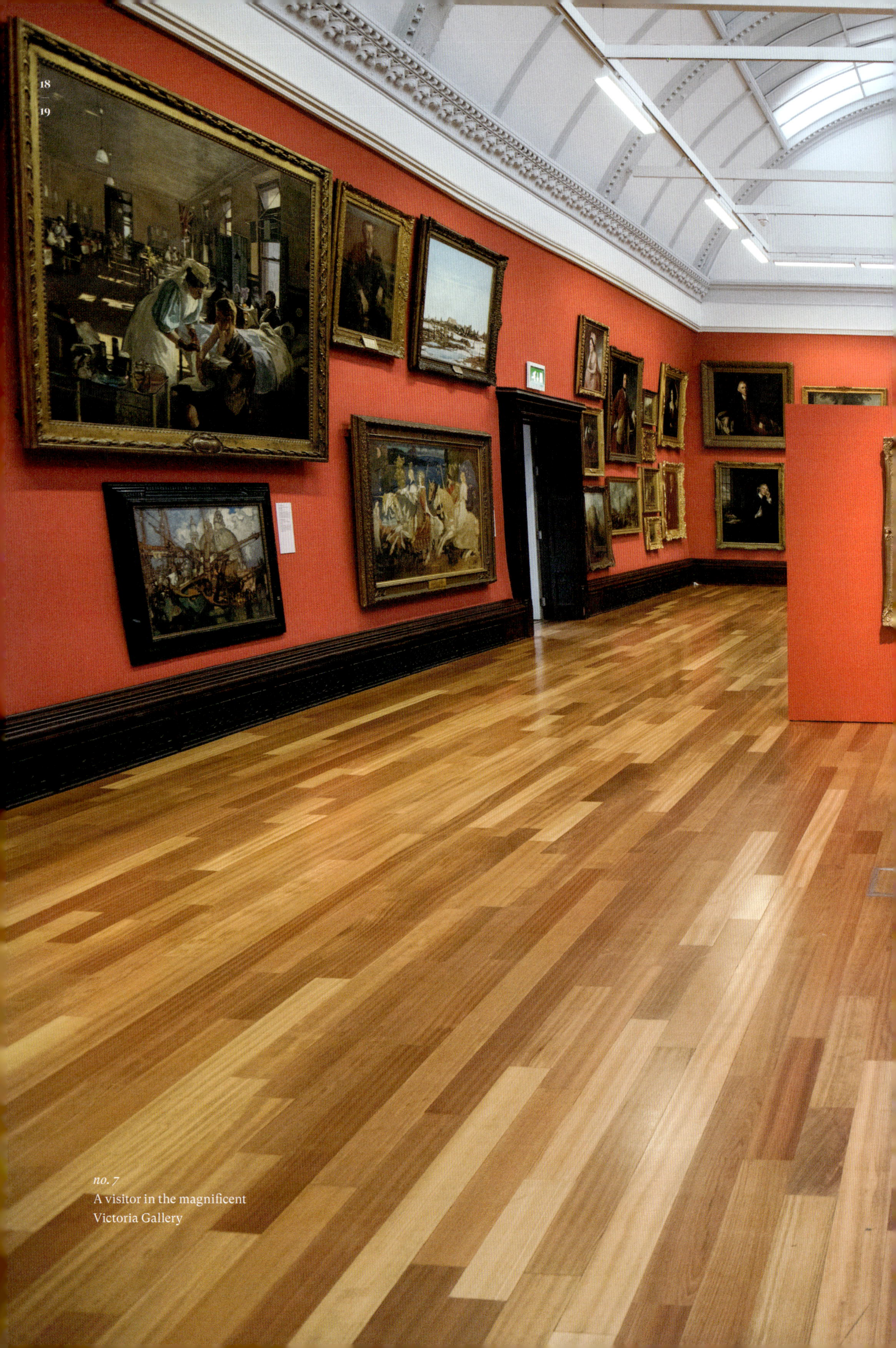

no. 7
A visitor in the magnificent
Victoria Gallery

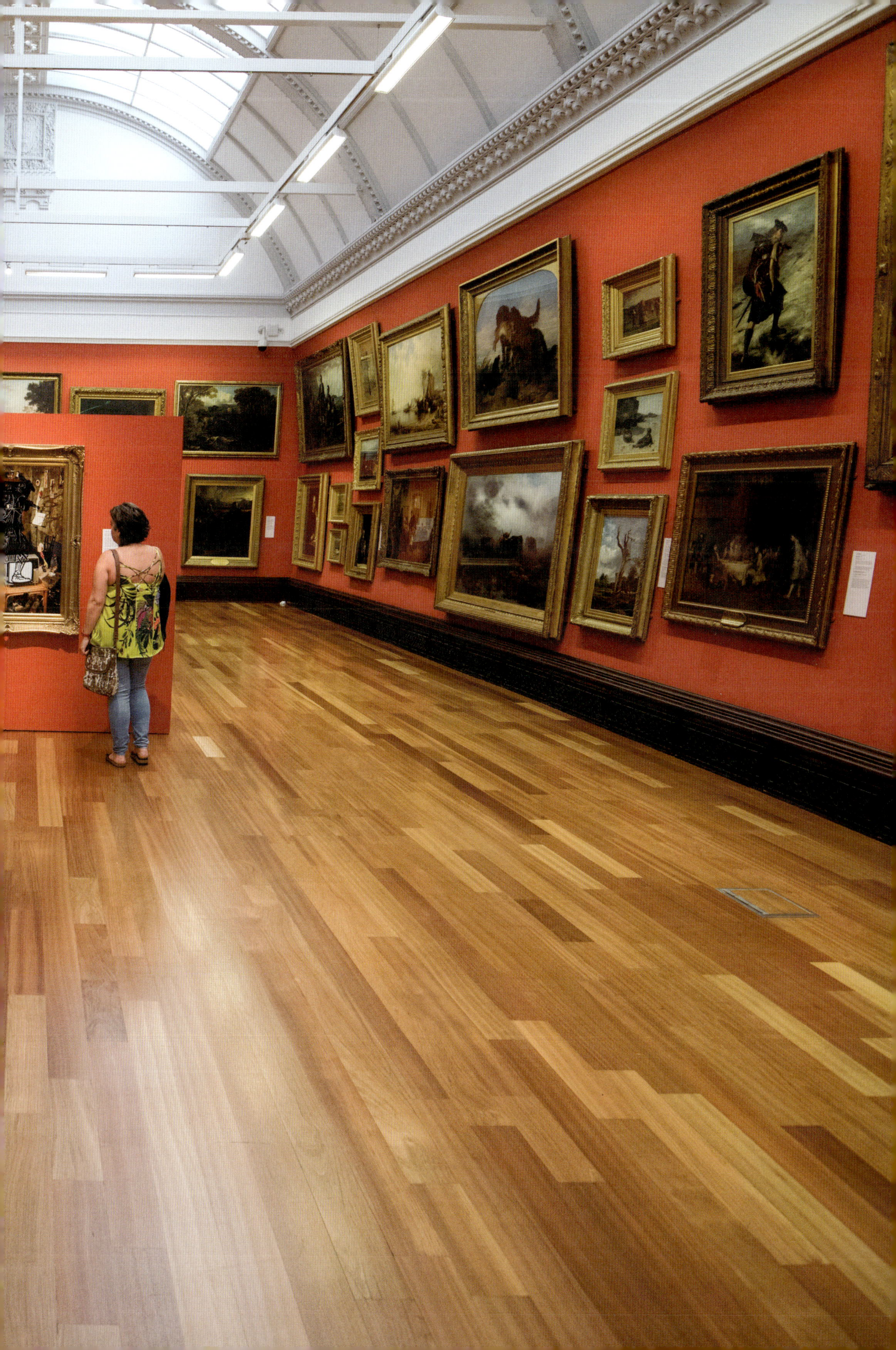

Billy Gartley

Head of Cultural Services
Leisure and Culture Dundee

Dundee: A City in Transition (1966) Joseph McKenzie

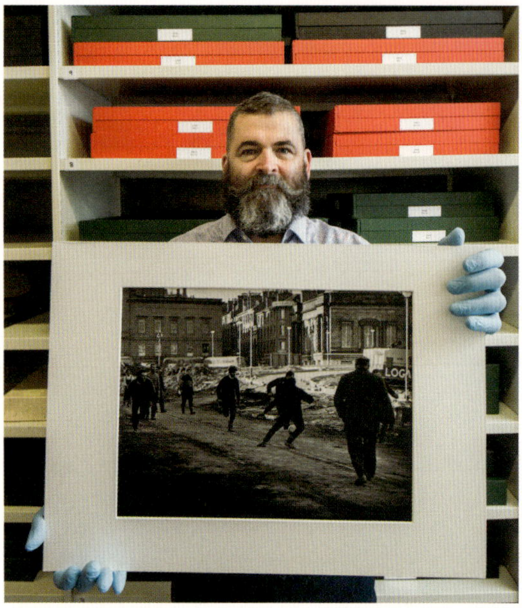

I moved to the city when I was 17 and visited the museum a lot – it was already a place of culture and inspiration to me.

I have the wonderful job of heading up Cultural Services, with The McManus as one of the three accredited museums that Leisure and Culture Dundee manage. Along with a dedicated team of Museum and Gallery professional and volunteers, we support and promote cultural and creative learning activities through curation, collection care and learning and engagement.

I moved to the city when I was 17 and visited the museum a lot – it was already then a place of culture and inspiration to me.

The object I've chosen is by Joseph McKenzie which is part of a series of more than 400 photographs called Dundee: A City In Transition (1966), a study he made to commemorate the opening of the Tay Road Bridge.

Joe McKenzie taught me when I was at art school in Dundee – he was a lecturer at Duncan of Jordanstone College of Art until he retired in 1986. He was known as the 'father of modern Scottish photography' and his work is held in collections including the National Portrait Gallery of Scotland and the Victoria and Albert Museum.

It shows a previous regeneration of the city's waterfront as workers take a break for a kick about whilst preparing for the Tay Road Bridge being built. The Caird Hall in the background is another Dundee cultural institution managed by Leisure and Culture Dundee so I have close ties with it today as well as fond memories from working there as a student.

This image echoes the current renaissance of Dundee and the changes that builds on, and celebrates the cultural offer of the city. I've seen thirty years of change now and that helped shape the celebrations for the 150th year of the McManus.

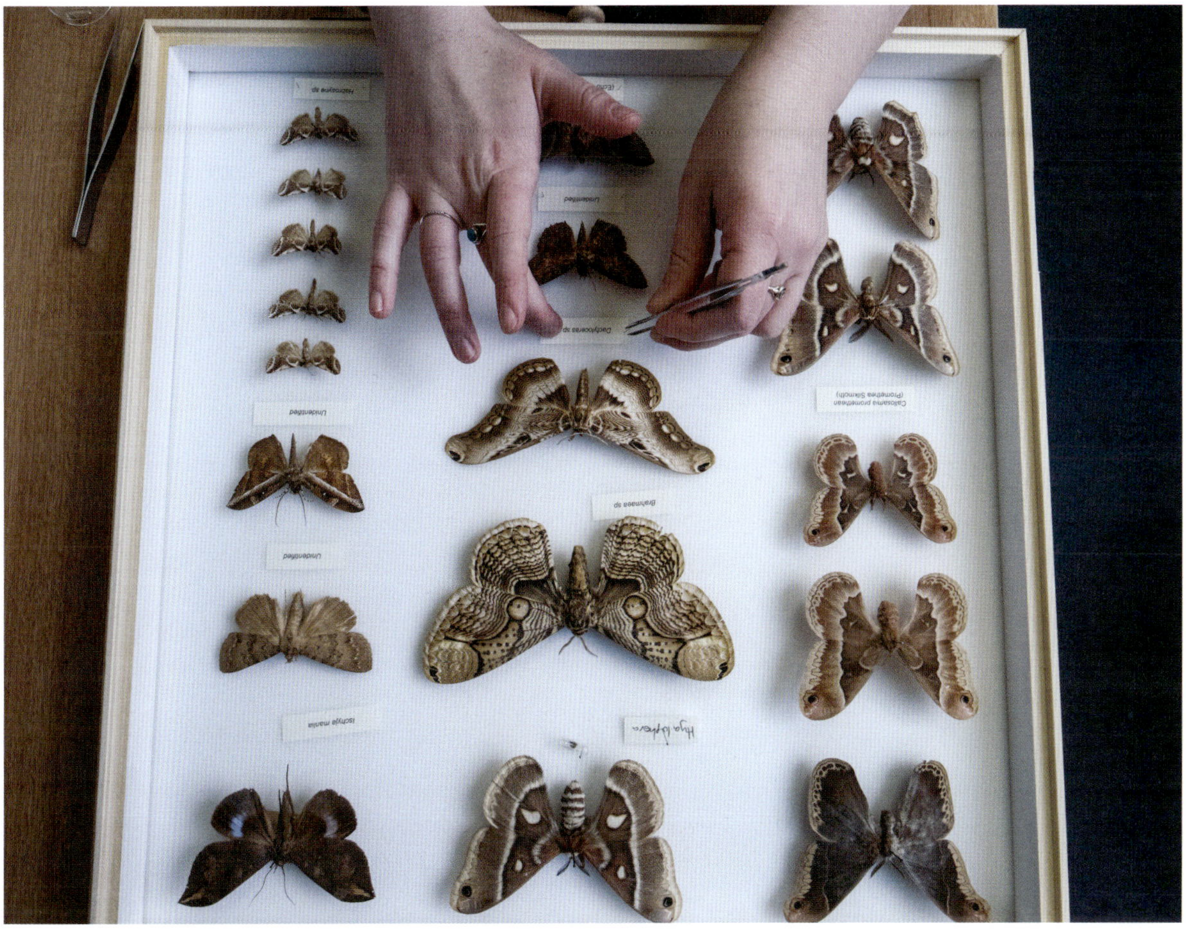

no. 8
Repackaging moths from the
Derek Robertson Moth Collection,
a project funded by Museums
Galleries Scotland

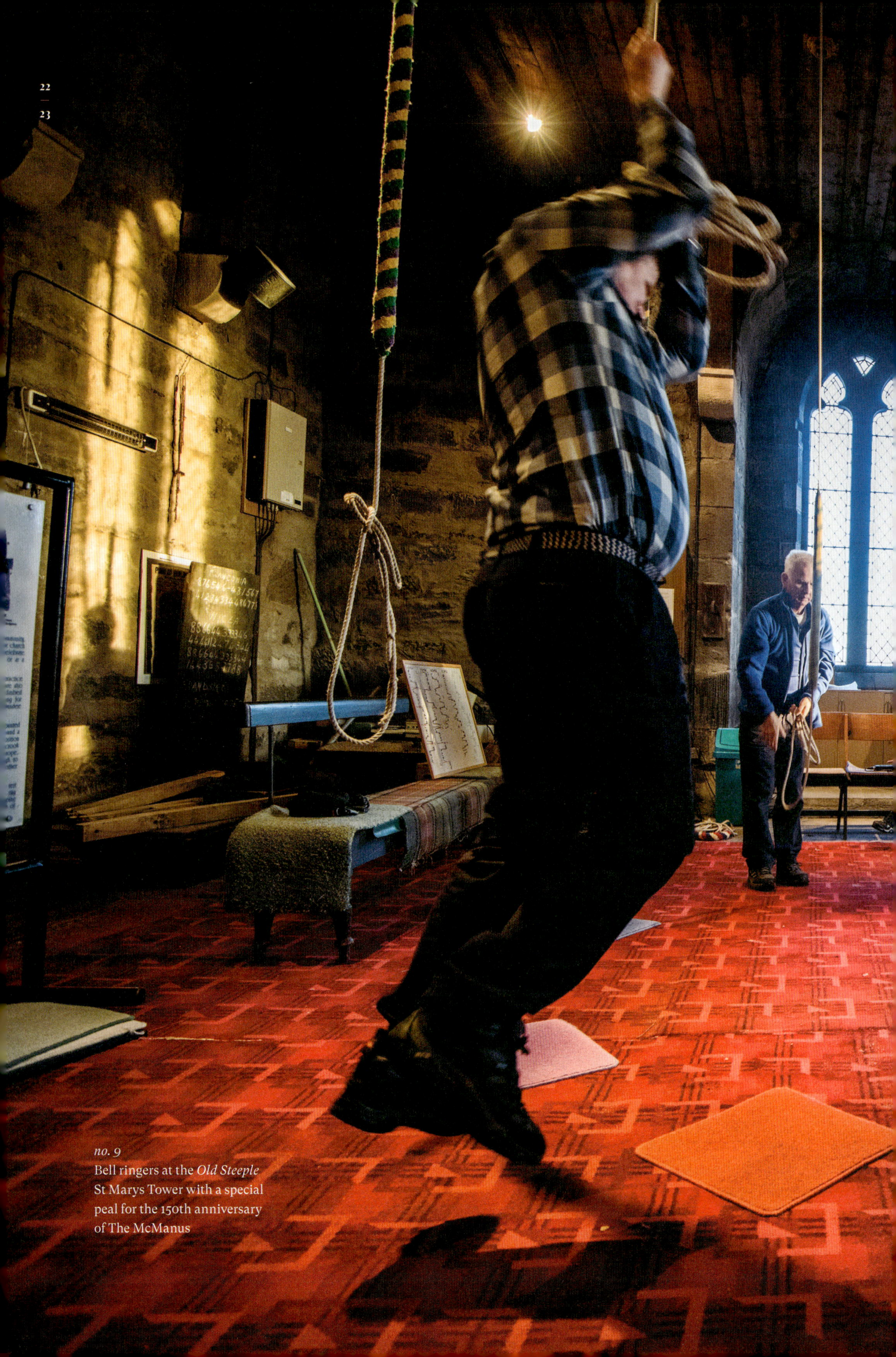

no. 9
Bell ringers at the *Old Steeple* St Marys Tower with a special peal for the 150th anniversary of The McManus

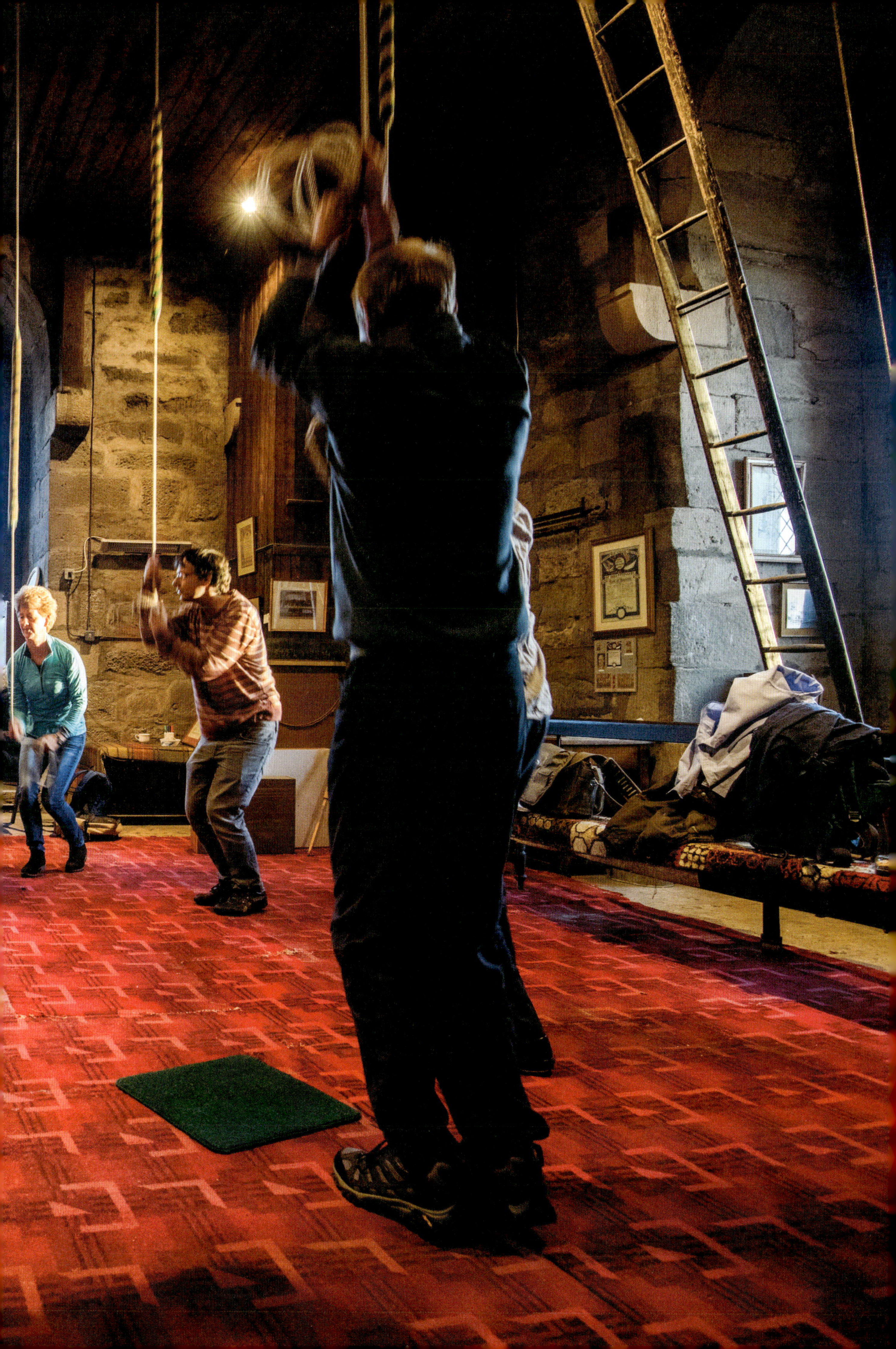

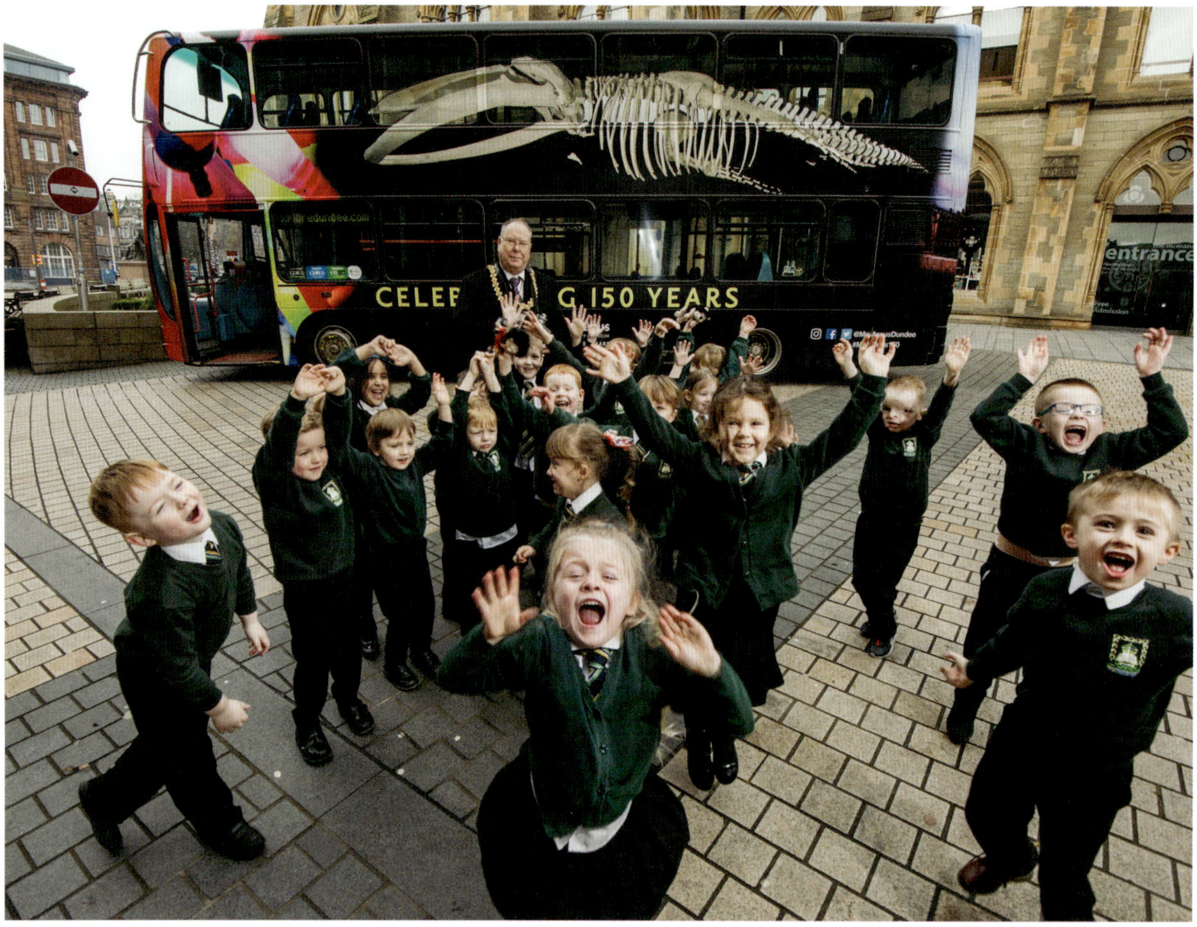

no. 10
Former Lord Provost Bob Duncan with schoolchildren celebrating the arrival of The McManus bus

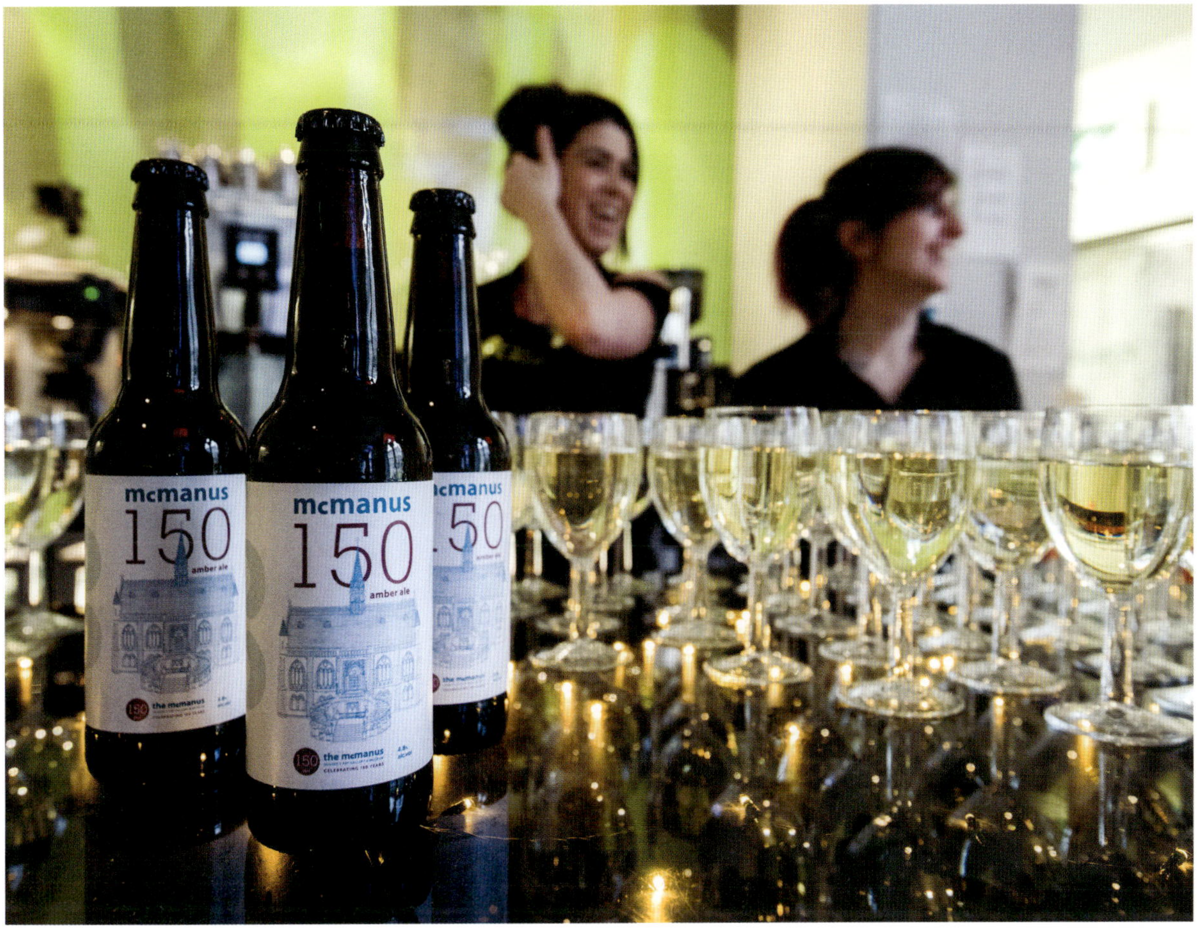

no. 11
The McManus Café staff with
McManus 150 anniversary beer

Alice Marra

Musician

Michael Marra
Calum Colvin

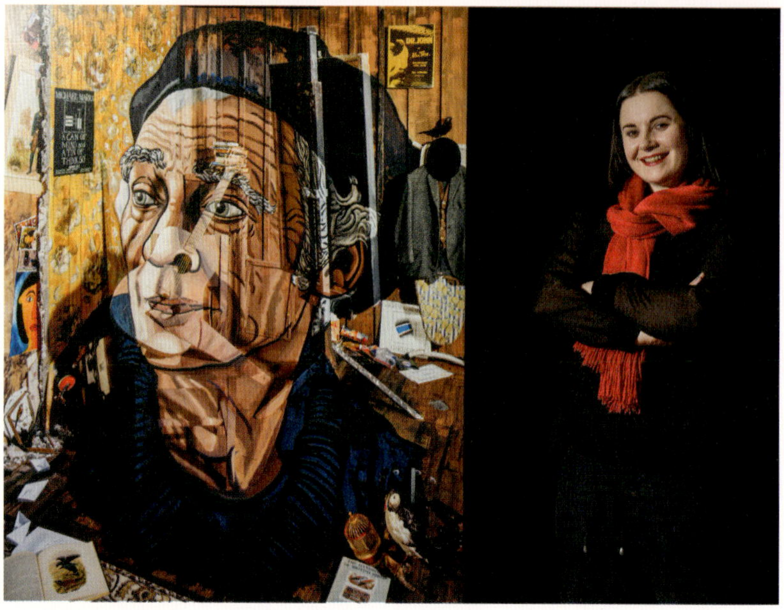

I remember it being a big deal, going to The McManus when I was wee.

I remember it being a big deal, going to The McManus when I was wee. There was nothing else like it in Dundee – and in many ways there still isn't. My mum used to take me on a Saturday; it was a real treat.

My favourite part was the shop and the pub – it instilled in me a love of social history, I'm still a huge fan of places like National Trust properties, or Beamish, where social history is brought to life. I have a fascination with how people lived. Now it's my place of work. I was asked if my choir would be the choir in residence at The McManus and we meet in the Creative Learning suite. But often we go out into the rest of the museum and sing in the galleries. We're so privileged to be able to use the building in that way and the art inspires us. I often see people wandering off mid-song, to look at the art.

One of my favourite pieces is Ron Stenberg's *Two Auld Wifies* painting – although I know it's not actually two old women. It reminds me of the blethering and friendship that happens when the choir meets. It's about more than the songs, it's a social event and important for the members. So that painting always makes me smile when I pass it.

The object that means the most to me is the portrait of my dad, Michael Marra. It was part of the Calum Colvin exhibition, Museology, but now it has been bought as a permanent piece for the museum. I hadn't seen it before it was hung as part of that exhibition. When I walked in on the opening night and saw it for the time, I took a huge breath; it was so surprising, somehow, to see this image of my dad. I went back when the gallery was quiet and saw it again and there's so much detail, I love it. Michael would be so incredibly honoured to have his portrait hung in this beautiful building in this city he loved. And not many people can say that there's a portrait of their dad in the town museum!

Brian Taylor

Political Editor
BBC Scotland

The McManus: Dundee's Art Gallery and Museum

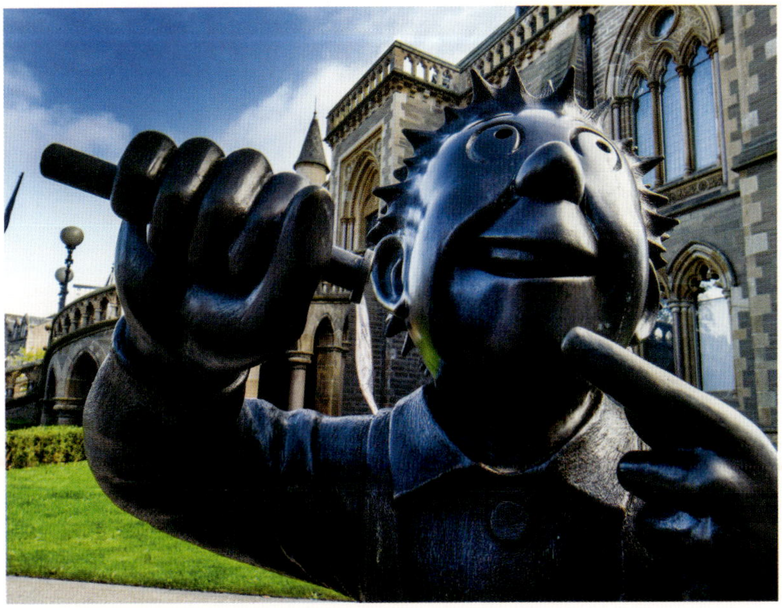

Dundee is an ancient, proud place – and it's great to see that pride in our history reviving.

Like many Dundonians of my generation, I will always refer to the building as the Albert Institute – although I commend its modern name. I went to school just across the road and regularly used the reference library. Indeed, it's where I sat for hours, writing my sixth year English dissertation. The memories of going up and down that fantastic spiral staircase, the awesome architecture. There's such a sense of grandeur, linked to the lengthy history of the city, as witnessed by the huge variety of contents. We should never forget that Dundee is an ancient, proud place – and it's great to see that pride in our history reviving. Even today, you can visit closes off the Nethergate or the City Churches or even the Howff to rediscover that great history within the modern city. The McManus helps provide a sense of context for the story of the people and the place.

Dundee is jumping these days, after a spell when it seemed – to some outsiders, at least – to be a wee bit in the doldrums. I think folk in the great and noble city of Dundee have simply decided that enough is enough and collectively have come together to improve the city, to vaunt the city, as have civic leaders, the universities and private business. Above all, perhaps, the vibrant arts scene is driving that renaissance: the Rep, the DCA and, of course, The McManus at the very heart.

I visit Dundee regularly. (OK, it's mostly Tannadice Park.) But on a recent sojourn, I was staying in the Queens Hotel. Nothing would do but to pester my puzzled BBC colleagues by quoting William Topaz McGonagall on the theme of Dundee. "And for stately buildings there's none can excel, The beautiful Albert Institute or the Queen's Hotel". Renamed the institute may be – but it is still gloriously beautiful.

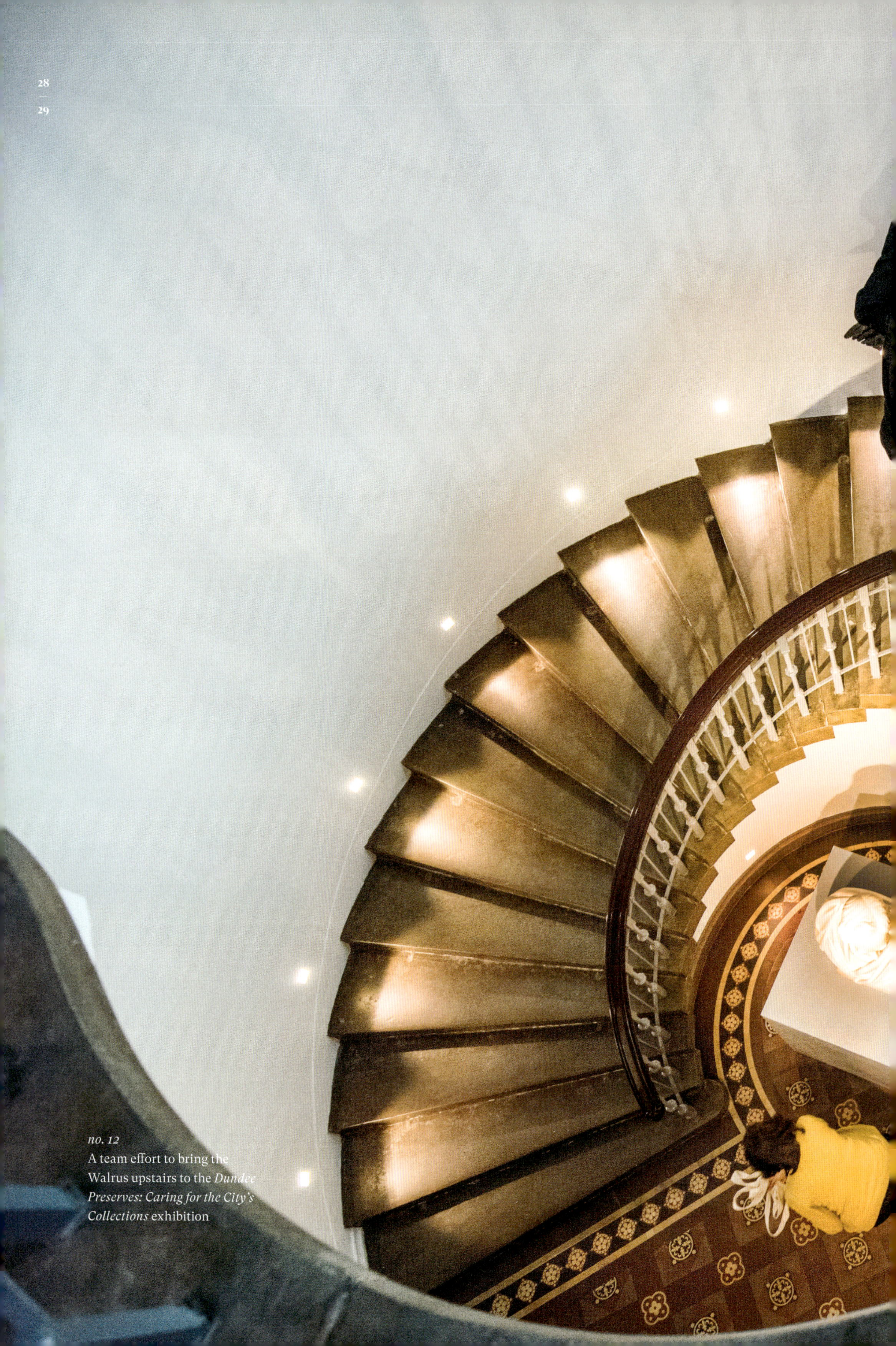

no. 12
A team effort to bring the Walrus upstairs to the *Dundee Preserves: Caring for the City's Collections* exhibition

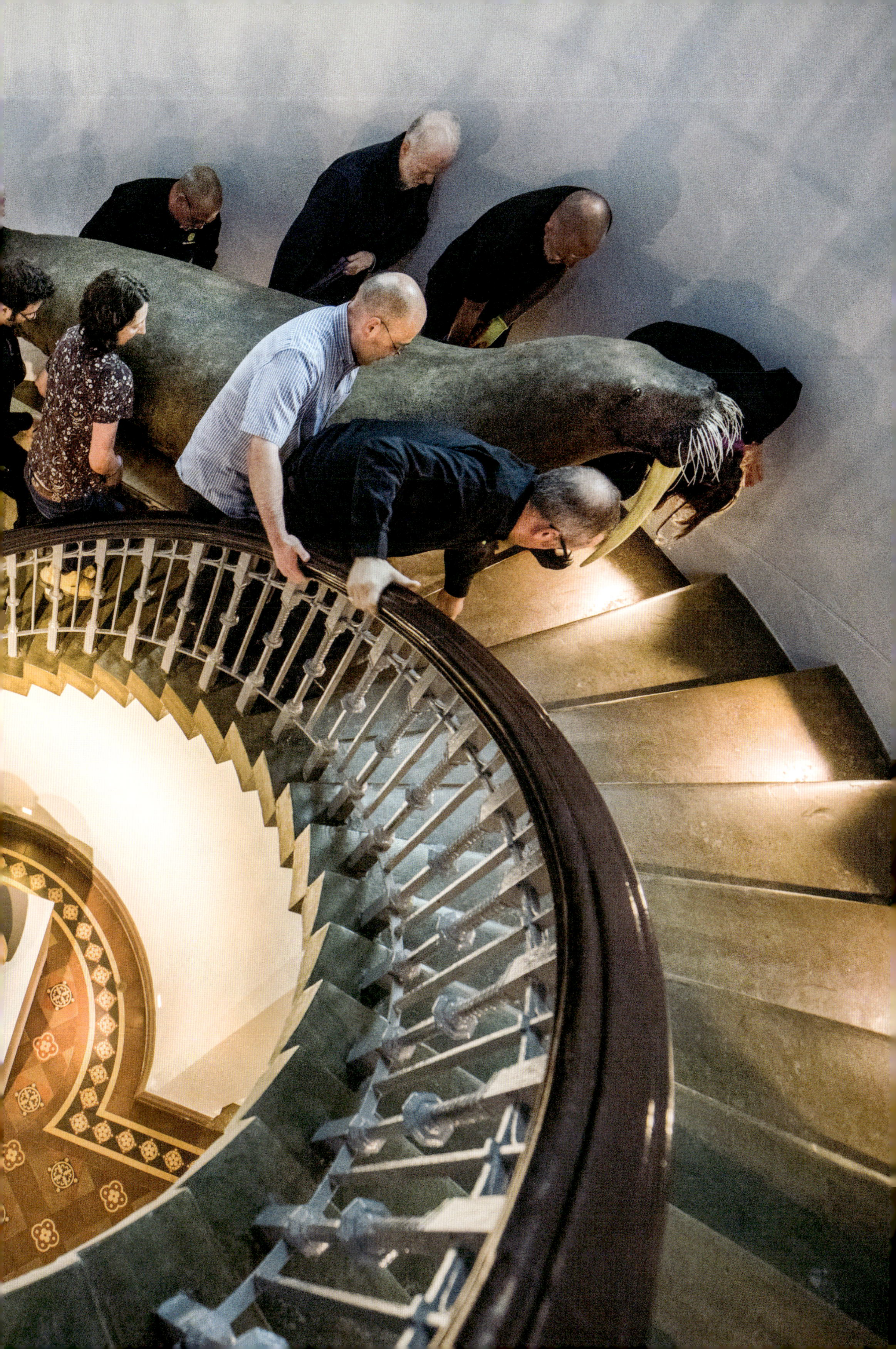

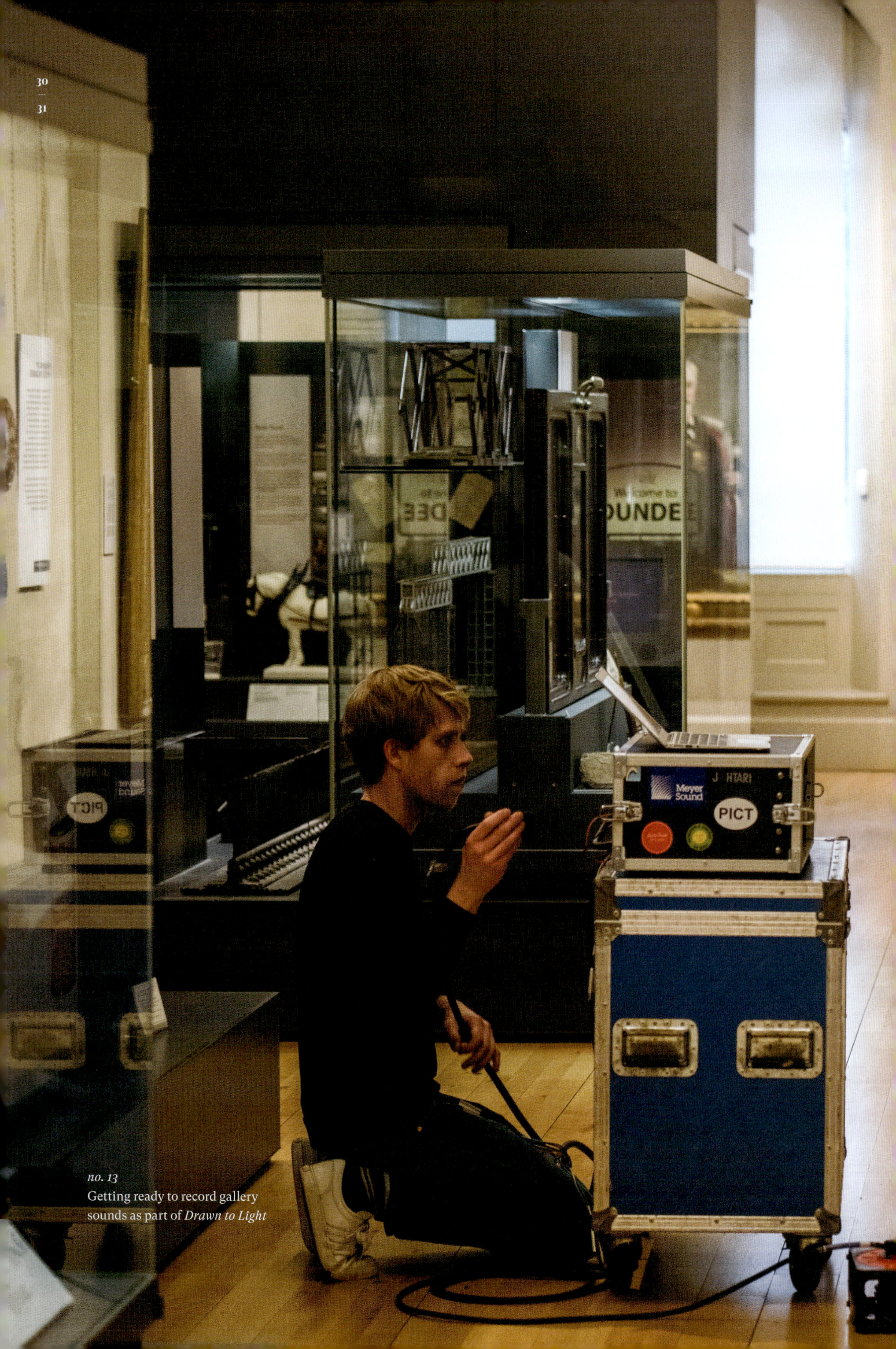

no. 13
Getting ready to record gallery sounds as part of *Drawn to Light*

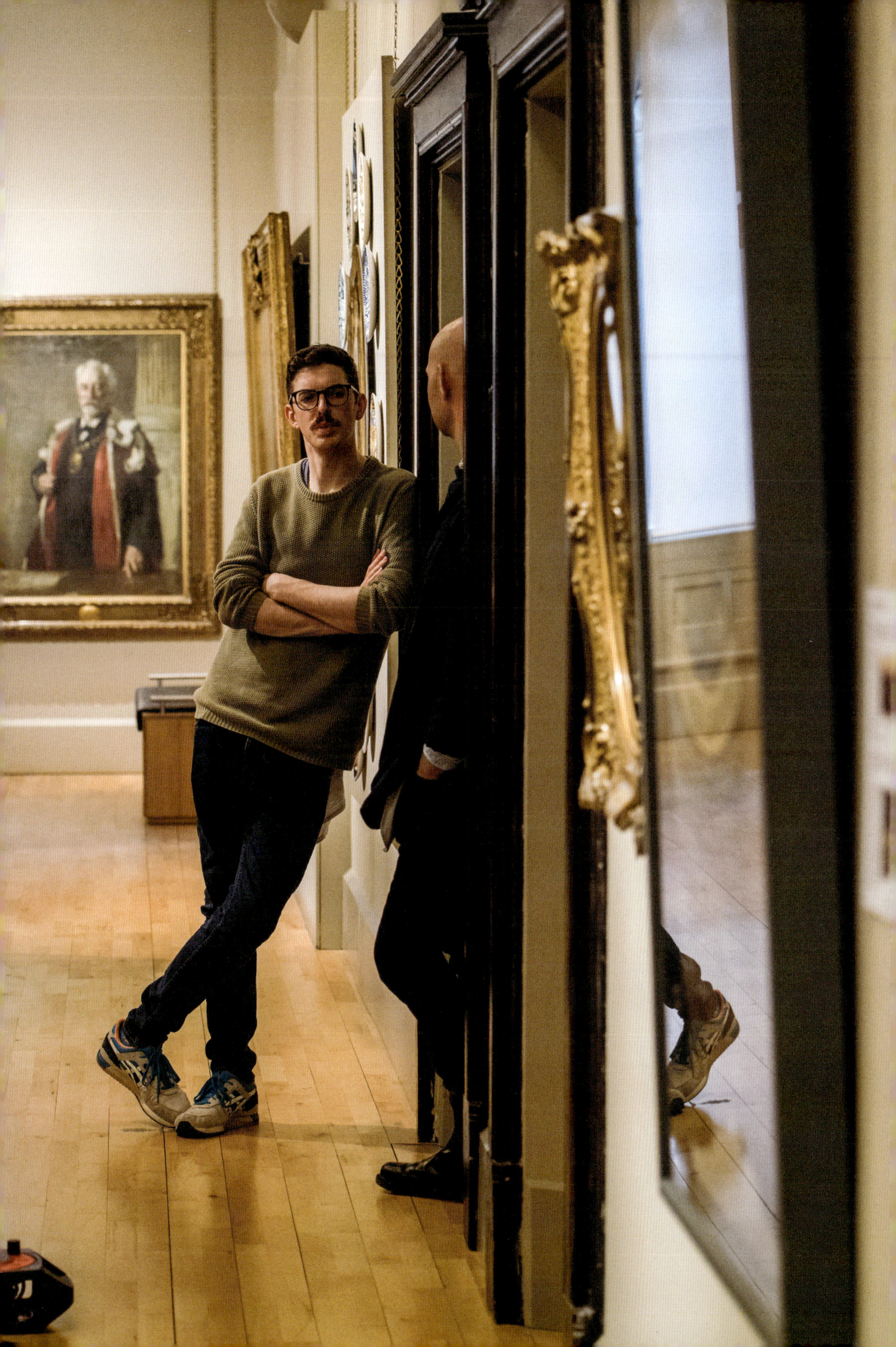

Moira Methven

Board Member
Leisure and Culture Dundee

Dundee and the World Gallery

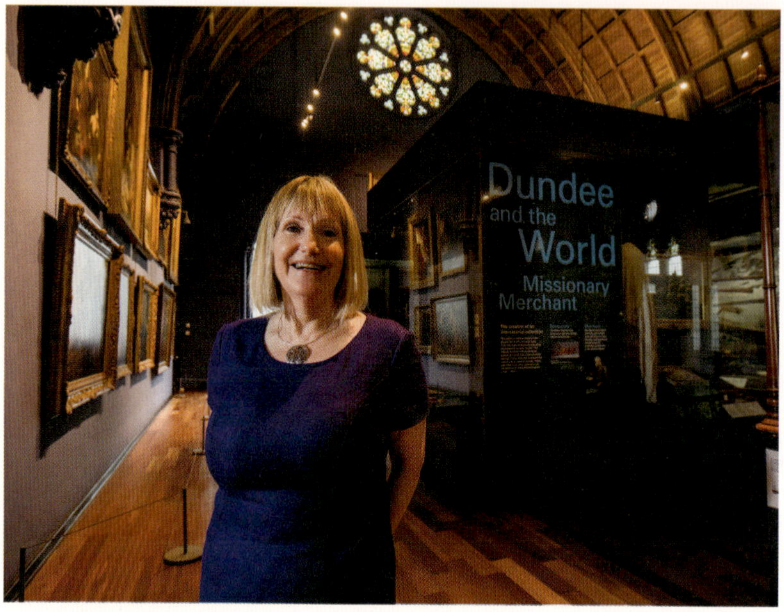

I loved the mix of people. That experience formed the rest of my career.

I've chosen the exhibition hall 'Dundee and the World'. This grand space has bookended my career. As a trainee librarian it was the first place I worked in what was then the city's Reference Library. A remarkable cross-section of readers streamed in – academics, school kids and elderly men (always men in those days) wanting to read the newspapers. The librarian had an encyclopaedic mind and would complete a number of crosswords every day, pre-empting the folk who would come in looking for answers. I loved the mix of people. That experience formed the rest of my career.

Fast forward to 2006 and as Head of Libraries and Museums, I headed up the project to revamp The McManus. The old 'Ref' had been gutted, leaving only the magnificent vaulted wooden ceiling and heraldic stained glass intact. Inevitably, given the enormity of the task, there was much blood, sweat and tears and many robust exchanges of views. Everything from light levels to the colour of the walls was given careful consideration. But the biggest challenge was deciding which objects from the vast collections would make the final cut. The city is lucky to have a visionary, committed and dynamic team whose hard work results in so many thrills and genuine surprises throughout the building. A real treat for both Dundonians and visitors to the city.

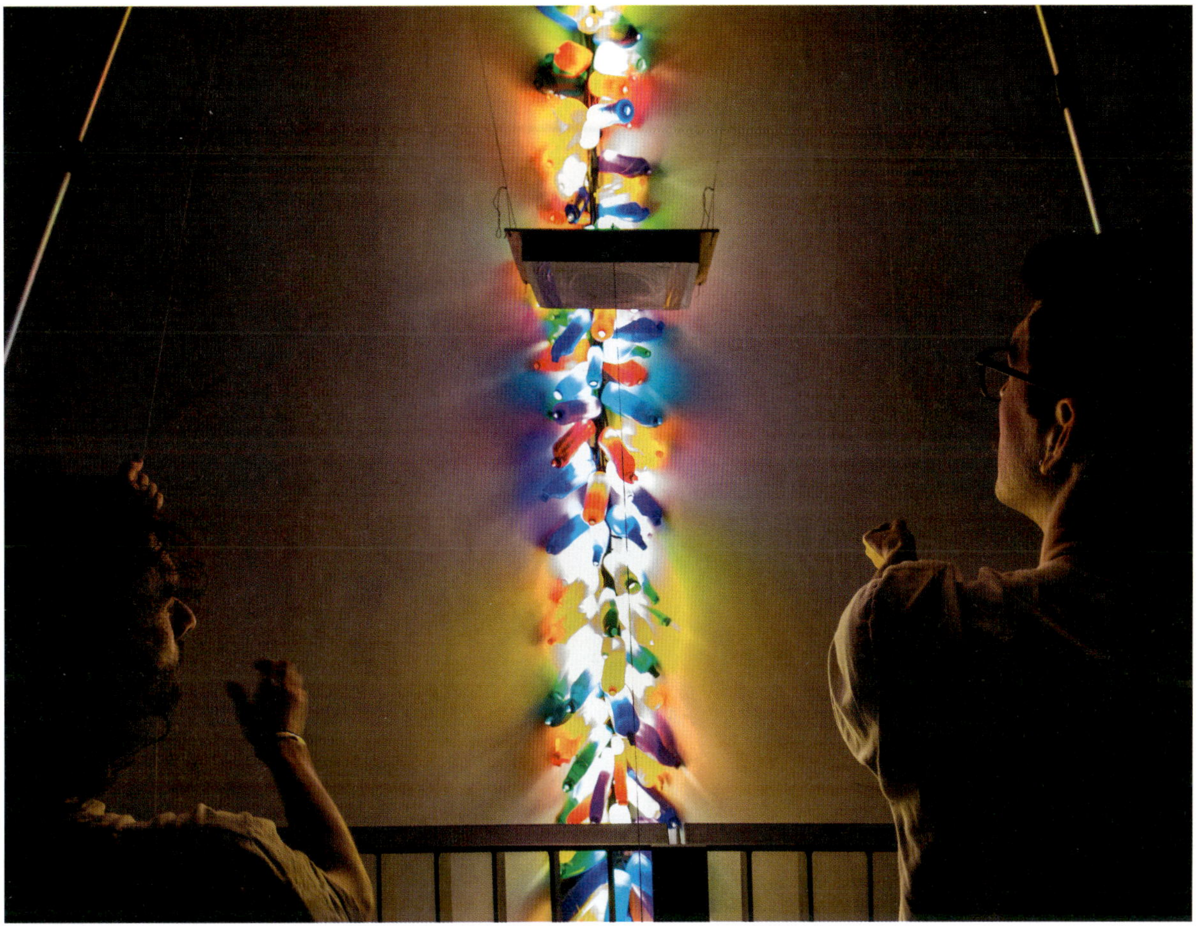

no. 14
Jonnie Common recording the sound
of the David Batchelor artwork
Waldella, Dundee

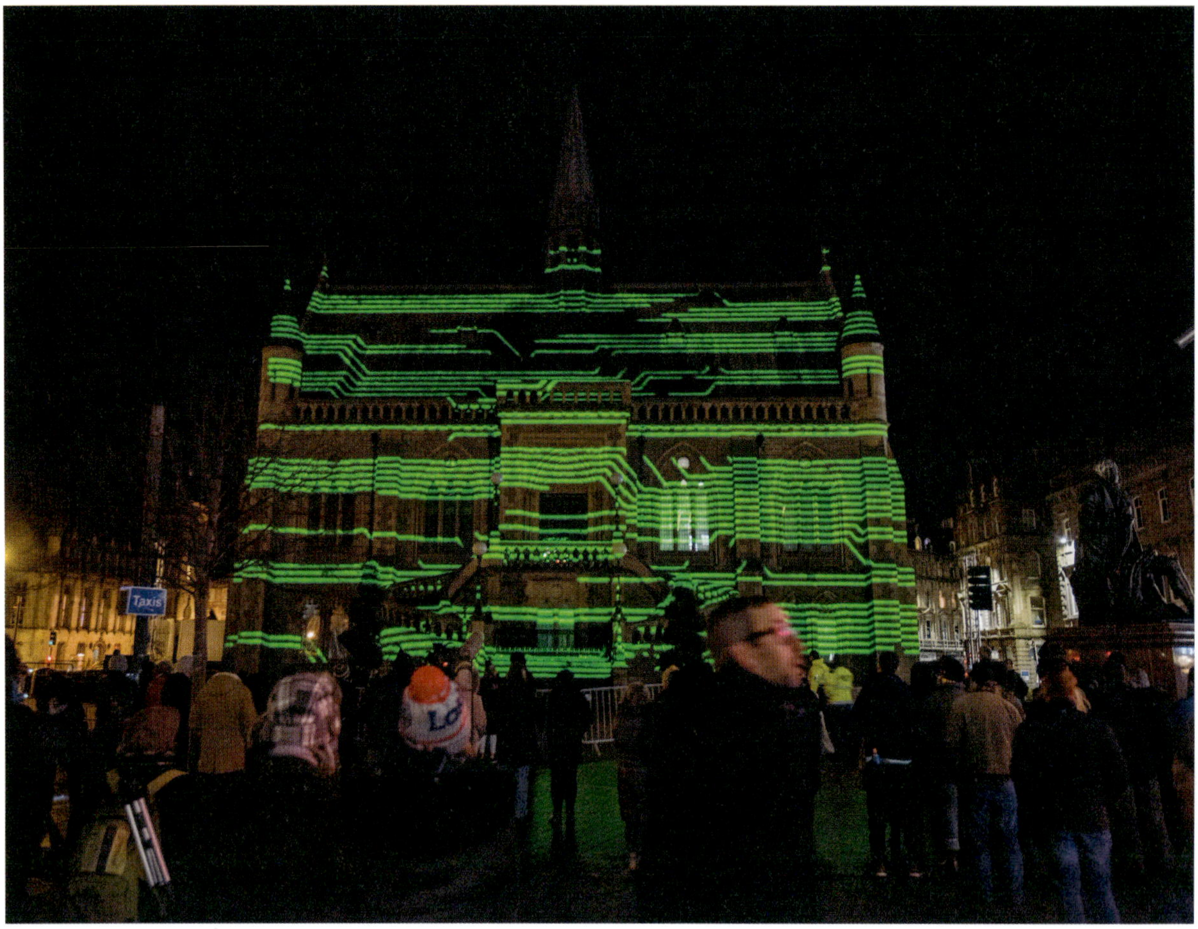

no. 15
Duncan Marquiss film projection on
The McManus *Drawn to Light*

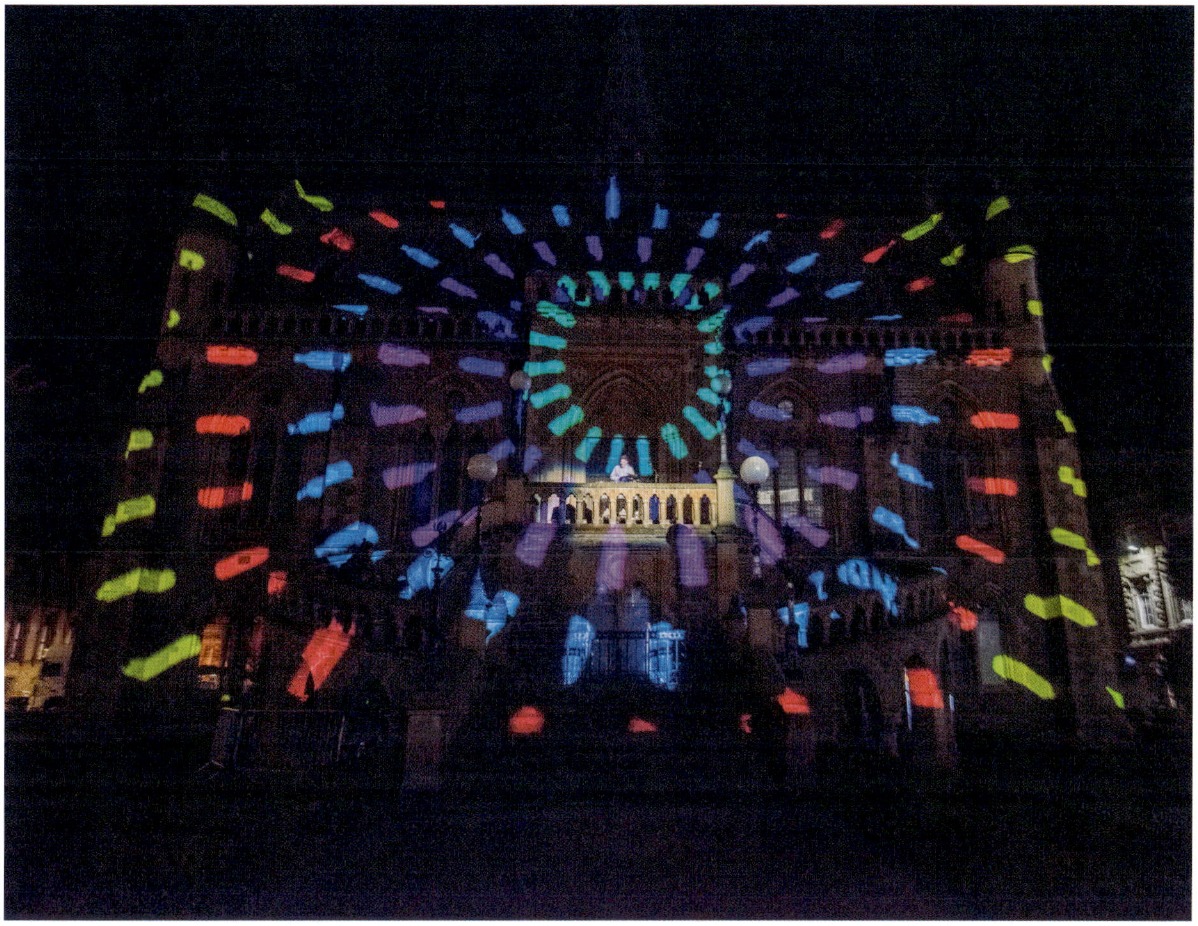

no. 16
Jonnie Common performs
with a nod to *Waldella*,
Dundee at Drawn to Light

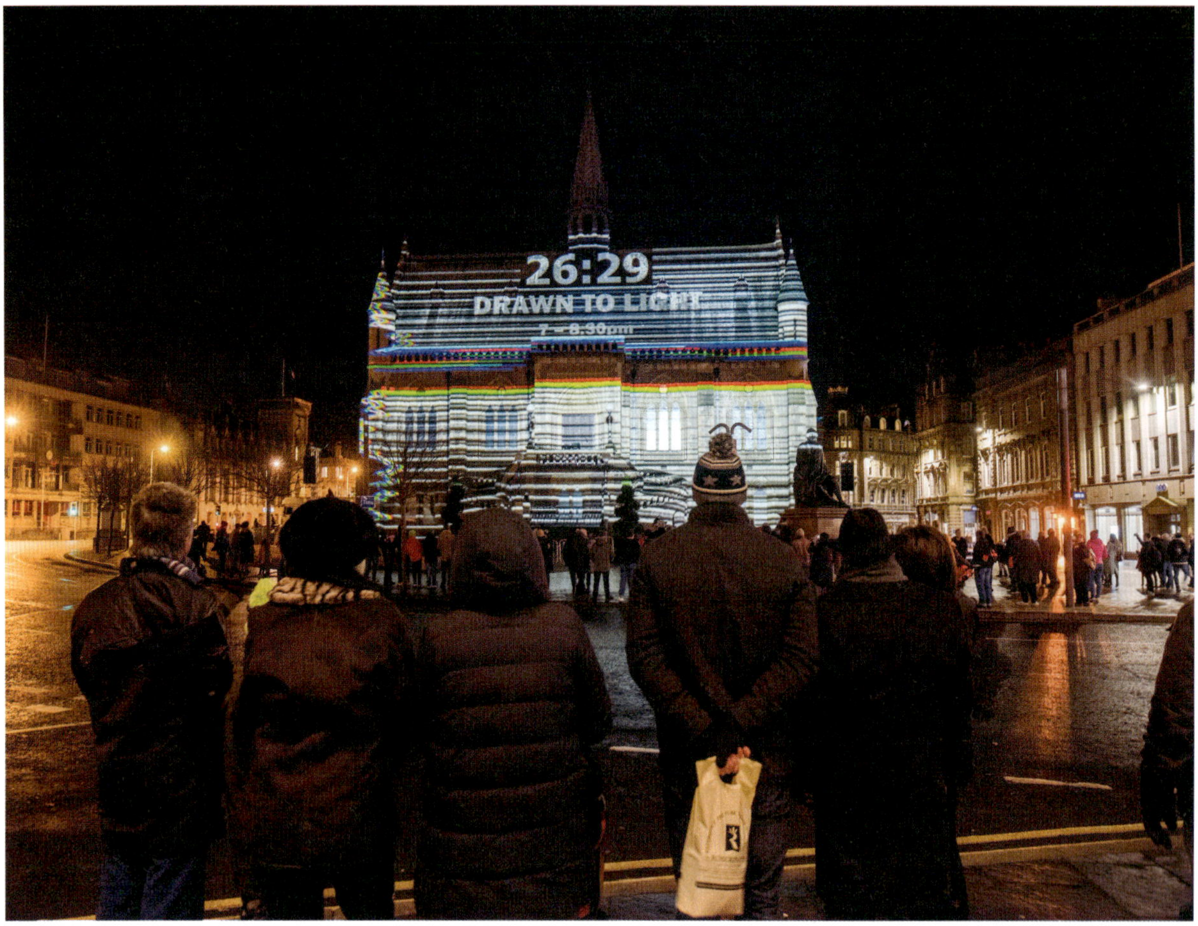

no. 17
Countdown to the beginning
of *Drawn to Light*

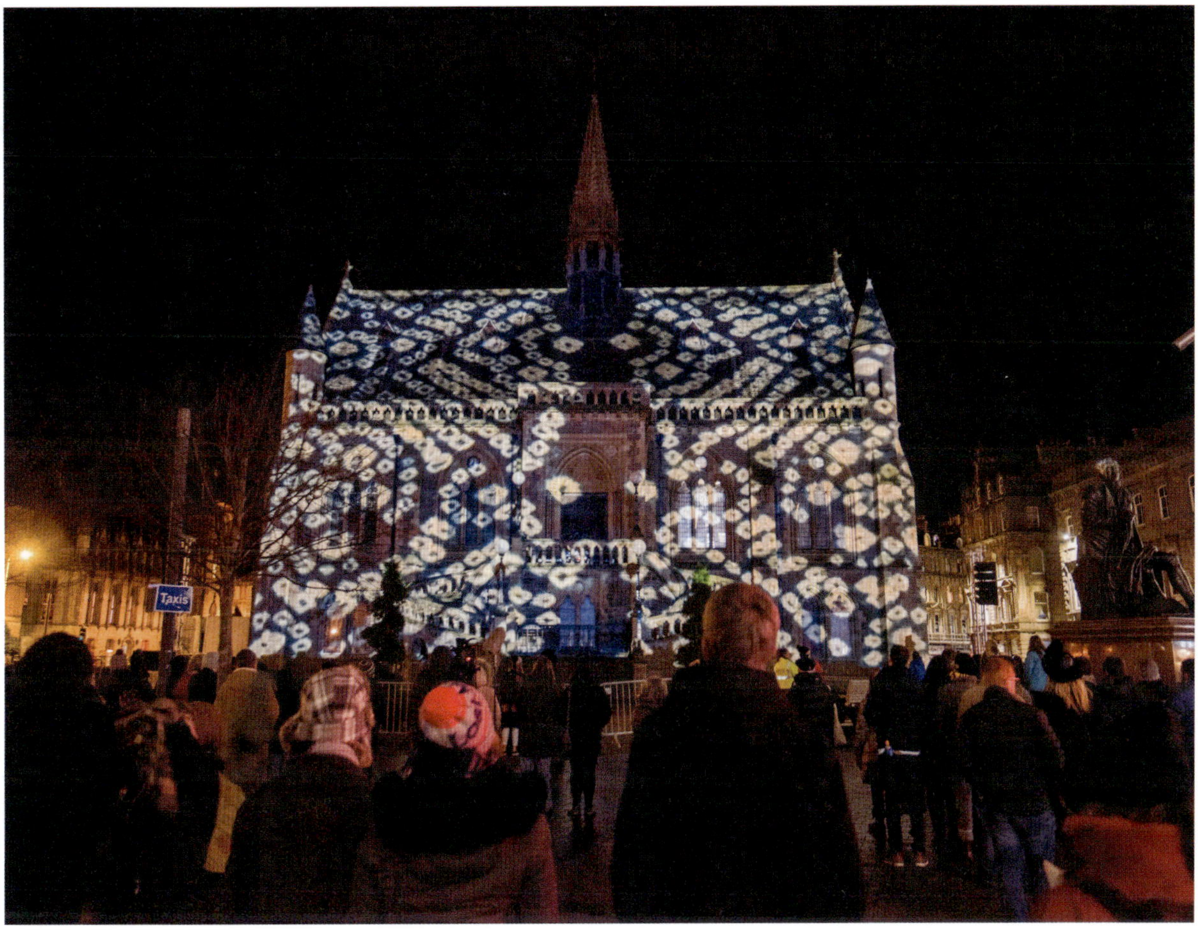

no. 18
Duncan Marquiss film projection
on The McManus *Drawn to Light*

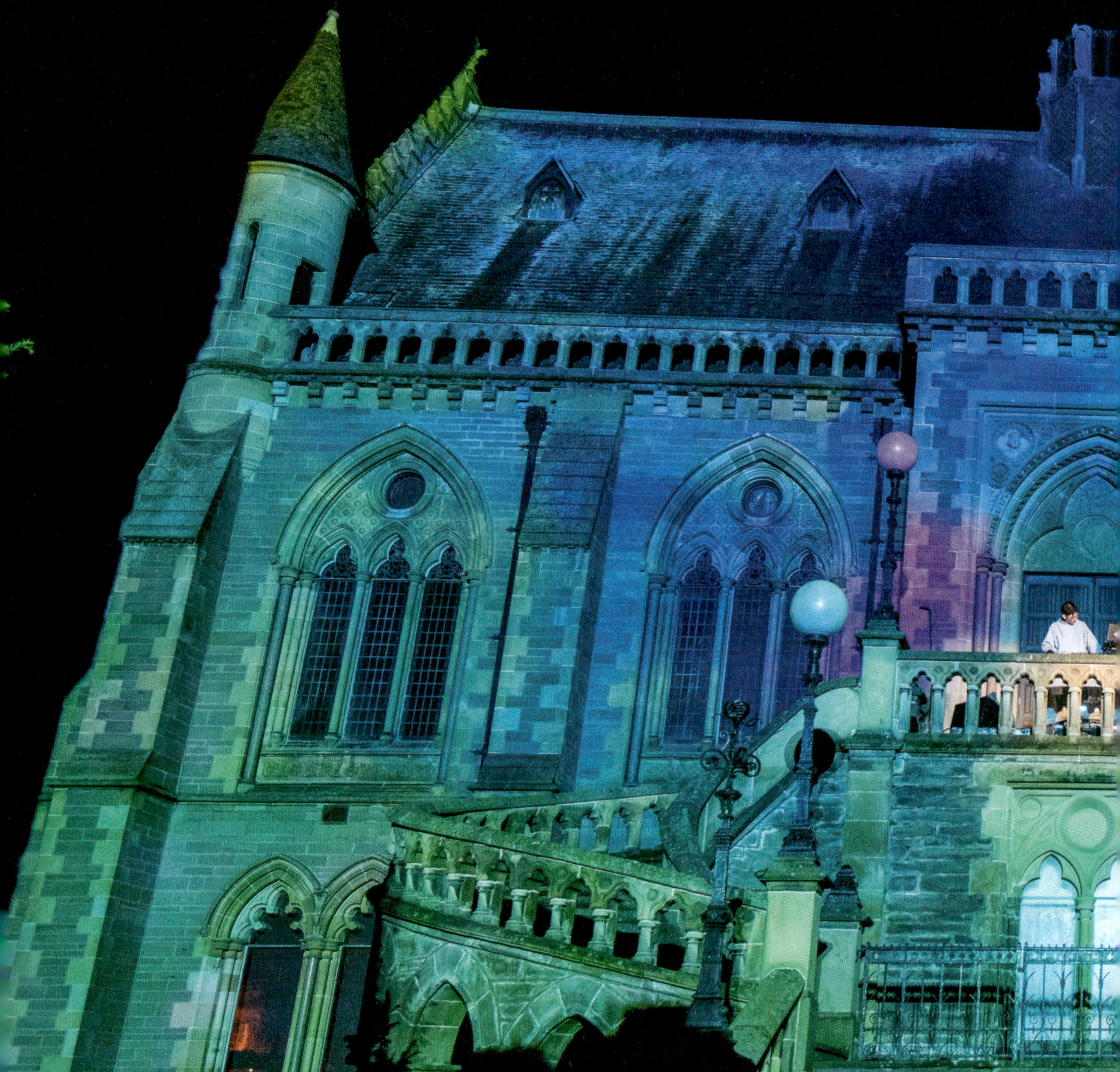

no. 19
Jonnie Common performs as part of *Drawn to Light* on the steps of The McManus

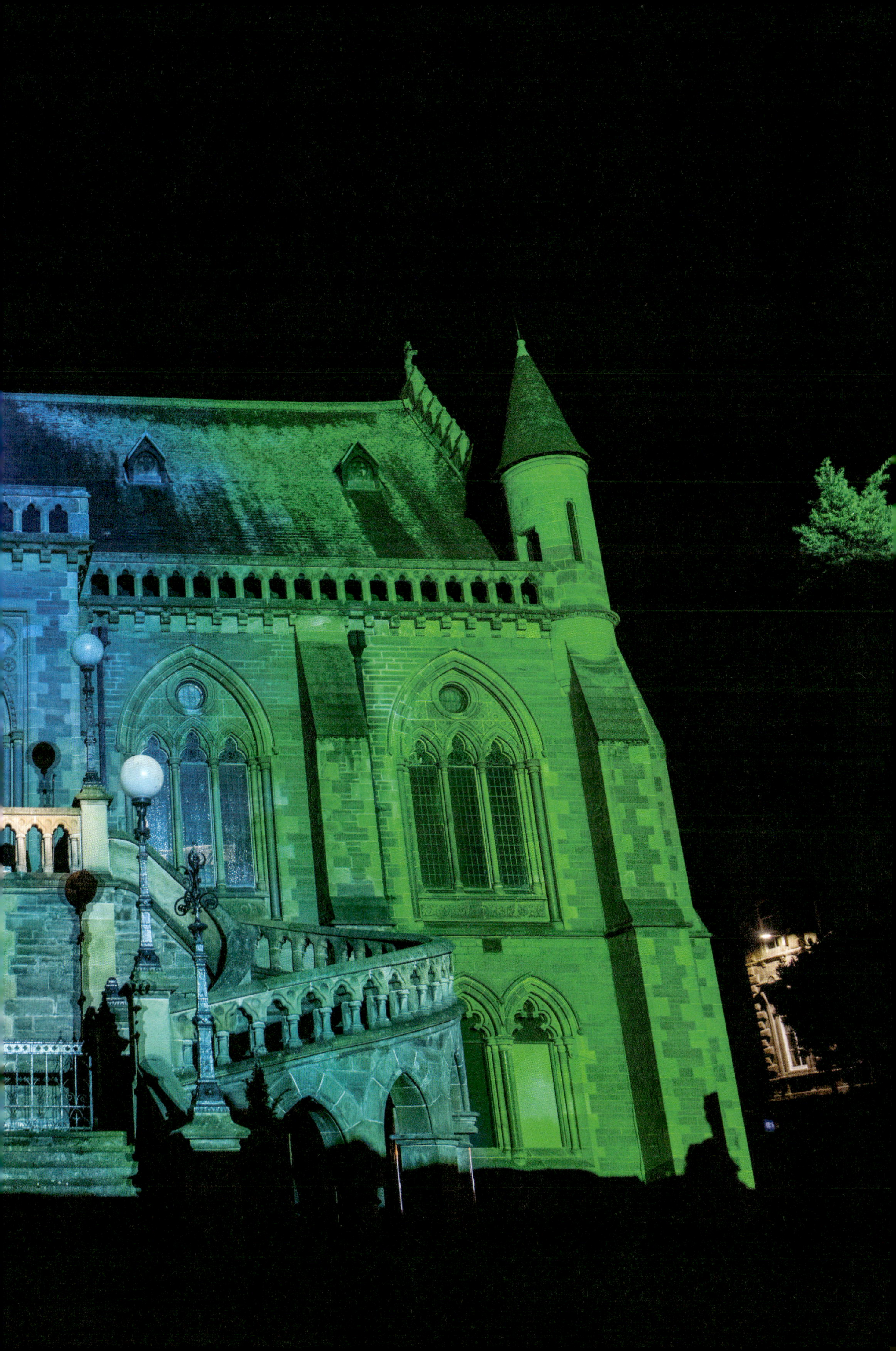

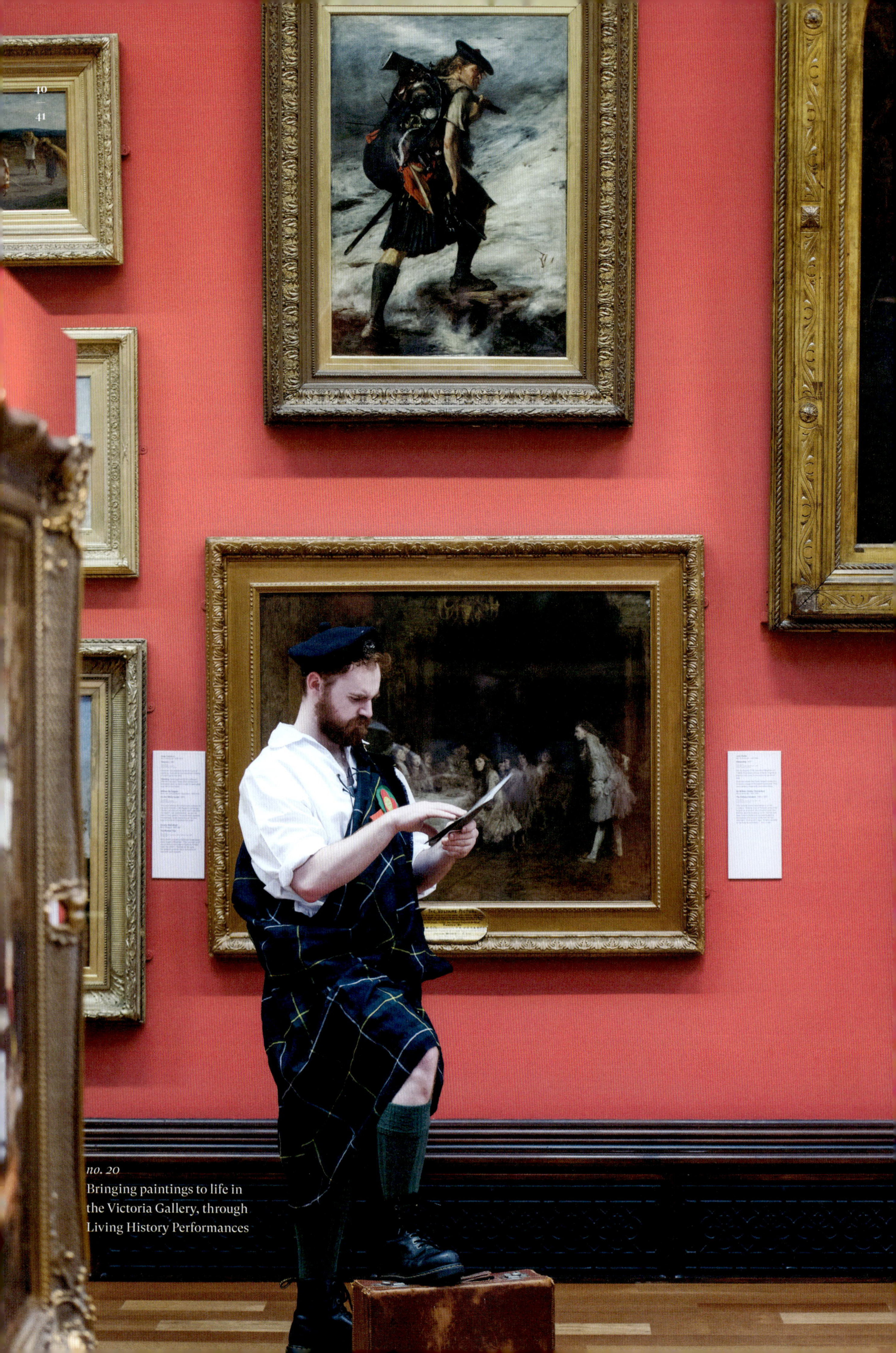

no. 20
Bringing paintings to life in the Victoria Gallery, through Living History Performances

Sinclair Aitken

Chairman of Leisure
and Culture Dundee

Disbanded, 1877
John Pettie

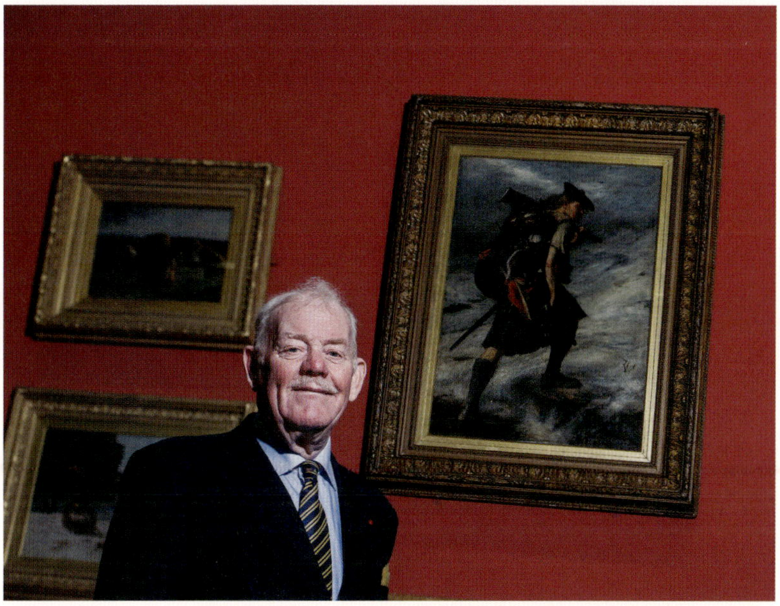

A light, airy, welcoming environment with helpful staff.

If there was a fire (heaven forbid), this is the item I would dash in to rescue from the flames. It ticks all the visual art boxes for me as, apart from the composition, it allows the viewer to make up their own story.

The Jacobite rebellion is a fascinating period in history. The modest numbers brought from France to support Bonnie Prince Charlie grew into an army that was only days away from entering London. It could have altered the history of the UK entirely.

The depiction of the Highlander, going home with his booty, suggests to me his weariness of war. I would like to think he left before the big defeat at Culloden because he was homesick for his wife and his family. I don't want him to be one of the deserters who left before the battle started. Obviously this was a bad day for the Scots who, despite a heroic stance, did not match the discipline of the opposing force. My man therefore was not a coward – more a survivor.

When I first came to Dundee I visited the Albert Institute (later to be renamed The McManus) and my memories are of a Victorian museum with dusty artefacts and a forbidding atmosphere. The change to a light, airy, welcoming environment with helpful staff has made the building a focal point in the city centre, with kids and families making use of the facilities and enjoying the many and varied items on display.

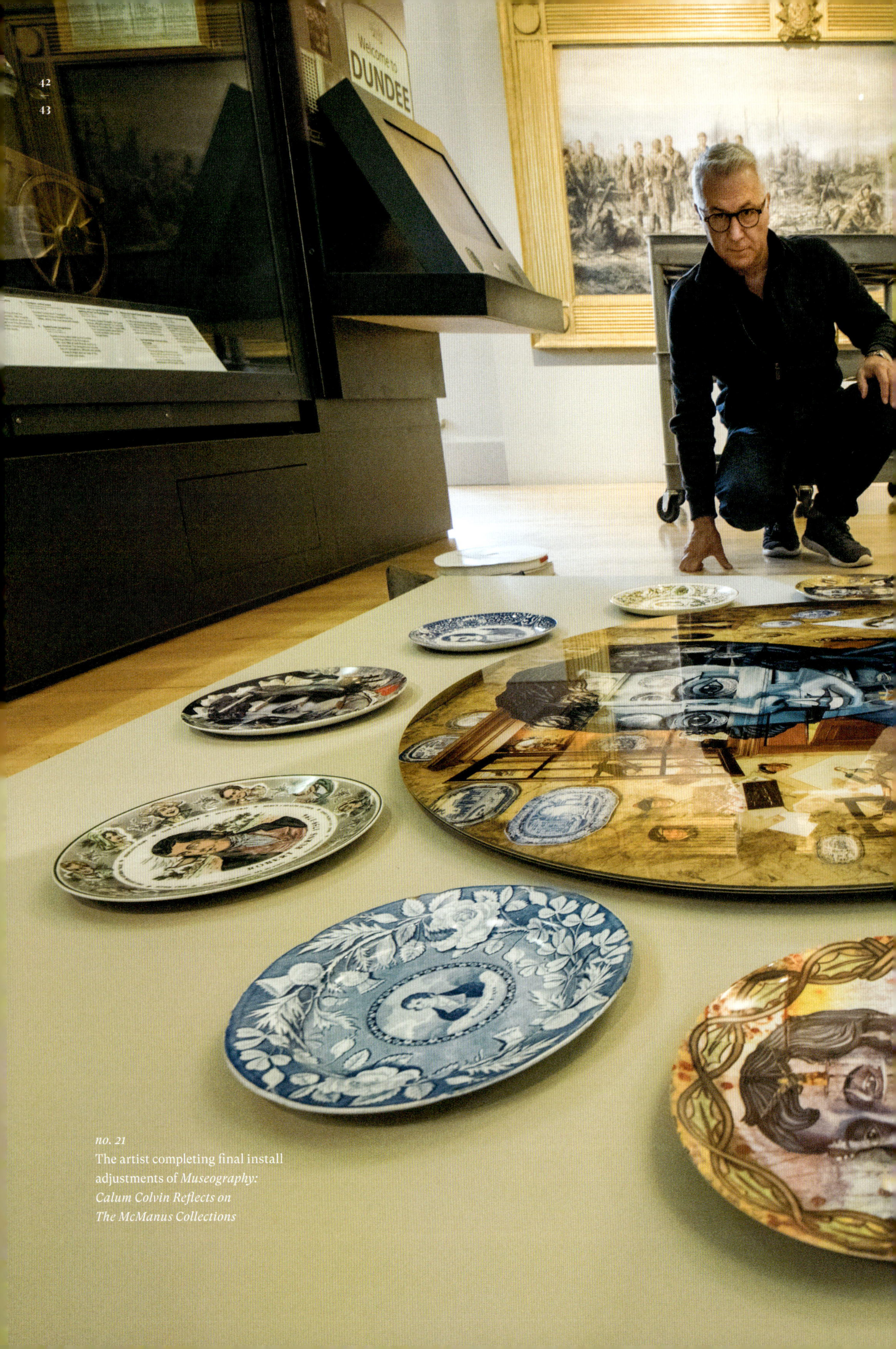

no. 21
The artist completing final install adjustments of *Museography: Calum Colvin Reflects on The McManus Collections*

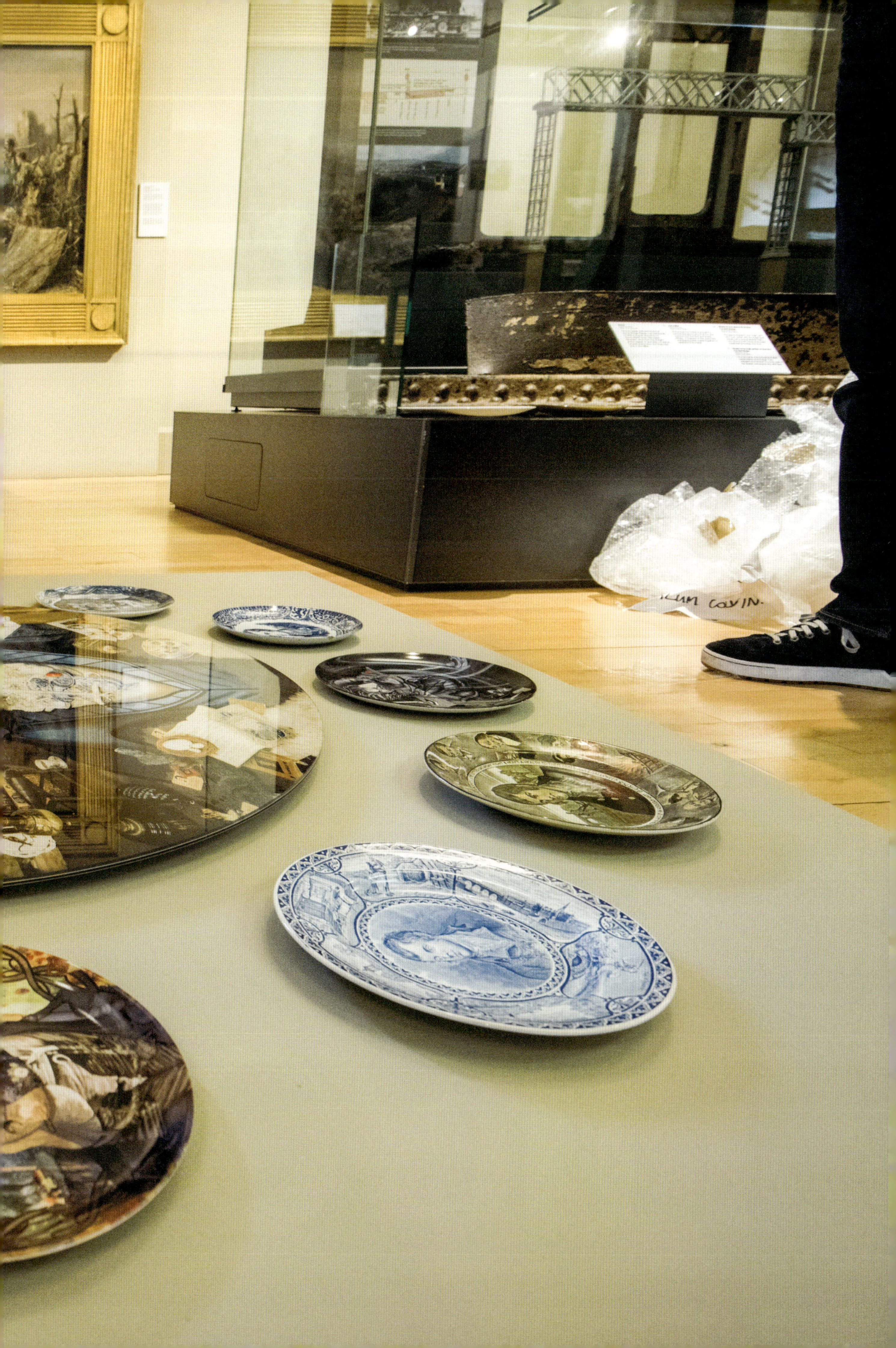

The Col

lections

The Collections

The city of Dundee's collection boasts an incredible 150,000 objects, but in common with all museums only a fraction can be on display at any time. The 150th anniversary of The McManus presented a perfect opportunity to use the collections, display them creatively and ask visitors to engage with them in an entirely new way.

Billy Gartley says, "During our 150th year we wanted an opportunity to show off our fantastic collections. We don't have the space to show all of them so we wanted to make the celebrations all about Dundee and how the museum reflects our history. It was also important to acknowledge the team that care for them and how hard they are working to preserve the collections for current and future generations."

The city's history, natural history and world cultures collections date back to 1824, with the foundation of the Watt Institute in Dundee. In 1869 these collections were moved into the newly established Albert Institute. A first extension to the building was completed in 1873 and by this date a small fine art collection had been established. Between 1877 and 1891, The Albert Institute became the venue for Dundee's hugely successful Fine Art Exhibitions. Purchases from these selling exhibitions, described as second only to those held in Paris, enabled the fine art collection to grow. Such was the success of these exhibitions that a third extension was required. Completed in 1889, this suite of four ground floor museum rooms and four first floor art galleries still form the core of The McManus displays today.

By 1895, the collections had grown so extensive that the Albert Institute and Victoria Galleries were overcrowded. The idea of opening a new museum, within the recently acquired Dudhope Park, was given serious consideration. The new Technical Museum was opened in the former Dudhope barracks, on the 23rd July 1900. With examples of model machinery, ship models, natural history and ethnography, its central feature was the Boulton-Watt engine, built in 1801 by Boulton and Watt.

The new museum became a very popular venue. However, with the outbreak of the First World War the Barracks were once again taken over by the military. Dudhope Museum closed in 1949 and the objects were returned to Albert Square. In 1978 the Library moved out to a brand new home in the Wellgate Centre. The Lending Library became the Trade and Industry Gallery and the Reference Library was reborn as the magnificent Albert Hall. The art galleries were modernised and over the next 25 years the building hosted a dynamic programme of exhibitions and changing displays. In 1984, the Albert Institute was renamed The McManus Galleries, in honour of Lord Provost Maurice McManus. In 1989, the magnificent Orchar collection became the centrepiece of a refurbished densely hung, red-walled Victoria Gallery. Displays continued to reflect the changing fashions in museum practice.

In 2000, despite showing its age, a dynamic programme of exhibitions and displays ensured that The McManus Galleries was voted Dundee's best-loved building.

Today, three of Dundee's collections are recognised as being of national significance by Museums Galleries Scotland on behalf of the Scottish Government; the entire Fine Art Collection, the Applied Art Collection and the Whaling Collection.

Anna Robertson, Fine and Applied Art Section Leader, explains, "Dundee's art collection is remarkable, spanning four centuries of production by artists working in Britain and Europe. At its heart is a much-loved collection of work by 19th and 20th century Scottish artists – with a strong Dundee flavour. It reflects the faces and changing topography of the historic city. It includes paintings that once decorated the homes of the wealthy jute barons, alongside prints that were accessible to all. There are artworks that challenge us to see the world differently and those that provide solace in often challenging times. It is a collection of constant surprises that we work hard to showcase."

The whaling collection is considered to be one of the most complete industry collections in the UK. Gareth Jackson-Hunt, Museum Services Section

During the celebratory year, one of the best received exhibitions was Dundee Preserves: Caring for the City's collections.

"As so few items are on display at any time, this exhibition allowed us to show off more than just the stars. For example, we've got 30,000 pinned insects – we got the chance to talk about them and really discuss their importance."

Leader, comments, "Whaling is hard to talk about, but it's a huge part of our history. Without it, there would probably be no jute industry. The two go hand in hand – and without these two industries it is arguable that there would not have been Levi's, not Timex nor its importance for the development of the computer games industry. This inter-relationship between industries is strongly evidenced in our collections."

During the celebratory year, one of the best received exhibitions was *Dundee Preserves: Caring for the City's collections*. This multidisciplinary display gave visitors a glimpse behind the scenes and engaged them in a discussion about what it takes to keep a collection in great condition. "It kind of spun traditional exhibitions around," says Gareth. "Usually when we do an exhibition we're very proud that everything is in top condition and looks perfect. This was an opportunity to show the public what we do behind the scenes, show more about conservation, documentation, how hard staff work to keep an item in great condition for 150 years. There's so much that goes into keeping the objects clean and this is one of the reasons why our annual Spring Clean is made so visible to visitors! This exhibition gave us space to show the visitors how simple things like light control, pest control and basic housekeeping are such an important part of our work.

"As so few items are on display at any time, this exhibition allowed us to show off more than just the stars. For example, we've got 30,000 pinned insects – we got the chance to talk about them and really discuss their importance."

Anna concurs, "We grapple to understand the significance of works in our care, if the information about them has been lost. In *Dundee Preserves* we showed a misunderstood painting in which artist and title had been misattributed. Research we undertook for the work to go out on loan revealed a significant early Scottish artist, subject and owner – all had a story to tell.

"Our visitors love peeking behind the scenes and we enjoyed being able to show the moment when conservation reveals an artwork hidden beneath layers of discoloured varnish. It was good too, to reveal that much of this conservation is supported by our partnership with the William S Phillips Trust Fund, fittingly established by the son of artist CGL Philips."

The city's early history collections contain some of the oldest surviving evidence of human activity. *Fire and Stone* focused on the Laws of Monifieth, with exhibits emphasising that the study of the past remains key to the creative urge today. With such diverse collections, it is easy overlook the fact that any single object is capable of being interpreted in a myriad of ways. To celebrate Dundee's new status as a UNESCO City of Design, the *What is a Museum?* display was given a design focus.

An early Dundee banknote, Dundee haute couture and the amazing natural form of a Venus Flower Basket informed and inspired in equal measure.

"Launching The Maritime Quarter which brought dozens of Ship Models out on display was a big moment in the year for us too. That exhibition is another that brings Dundee's history to life. A time when Dundee was really outward-looking and the world came to us. I think that still reflects where we are now, we're an open and welcoming city."

"Launching *The Maritime Quarter* which brought dozens of Ship Models out on display was a big moment in the year for us too. That exhibition is another that brings Dundee's history to life. A time when Dundee was really outward looking and the world came to us. I think that still reflects where we are now, we're an open and welcoming city," says Gareth.

"The 150th celebrations really did enable us to highlight how much we achieve with the involvement of partners", says Anna. "At the start of the year, we had work on display by Corin Sworn. Originally shown in Scotland + Venice, Sworn's entire presentation was gifted to Dundee by the patrons group Outset Scotland. Similarly the displays *Out of the Frame* and *Sense of Place*, focused on Scottish abstraction and Scottish landscape painting, were entirely drawn from the city's permanent collection, which was built as a result of the generosity of grant bodies and private donors."

The McManus collection remains dynamic with staff actively collecting the historic material you might expect, but also ensuring that contemporary collecting reflects our lives and the world in which we live. They collect to evidence the best of our national, and increasingly our international, cultural history and to preserve what's happening in Dundee – the ebbs and flows, the highs and lows.

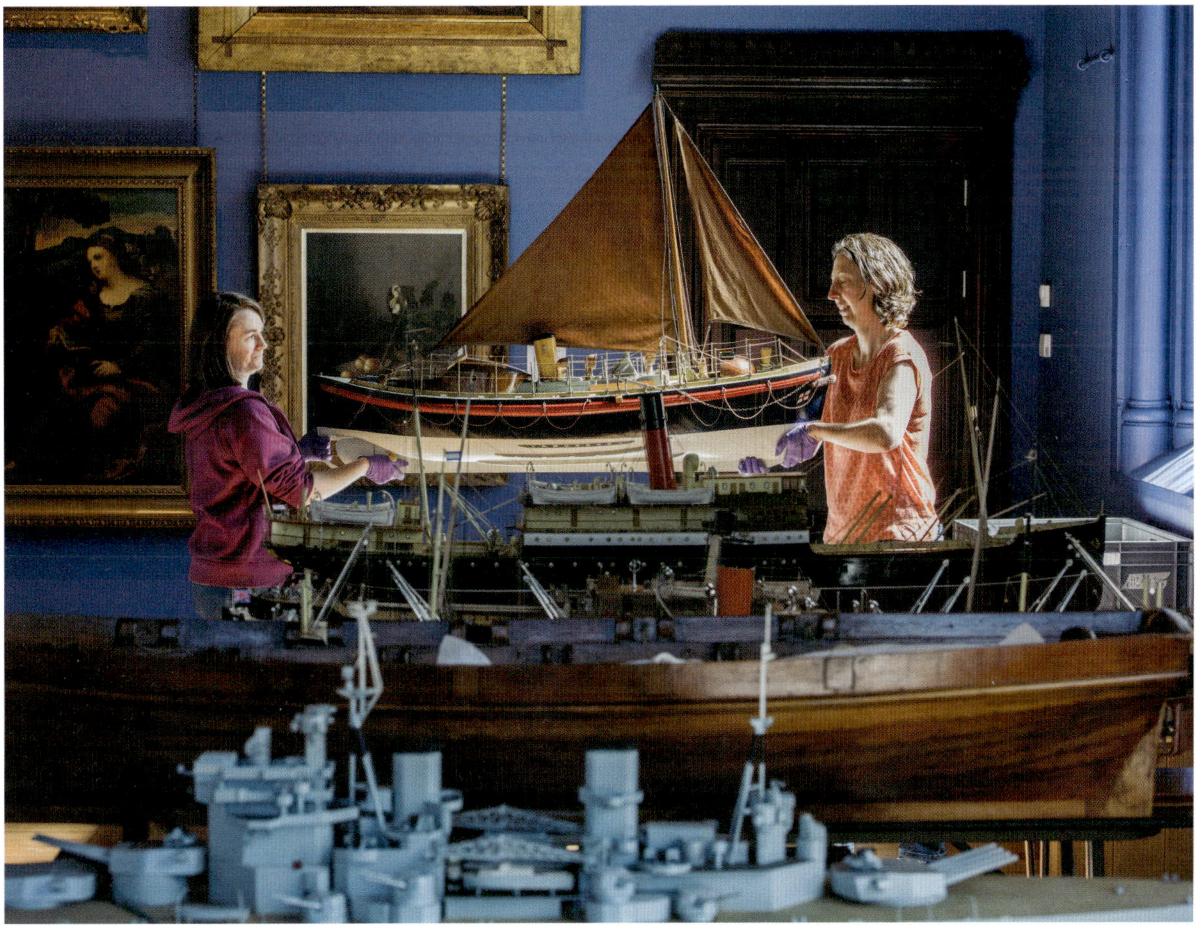

no. 22
Carly Cooper and Rebecca Jackson-Hunt moving the RNLI lifeboat model Mona to her new home in the *Maritime Quarter* display

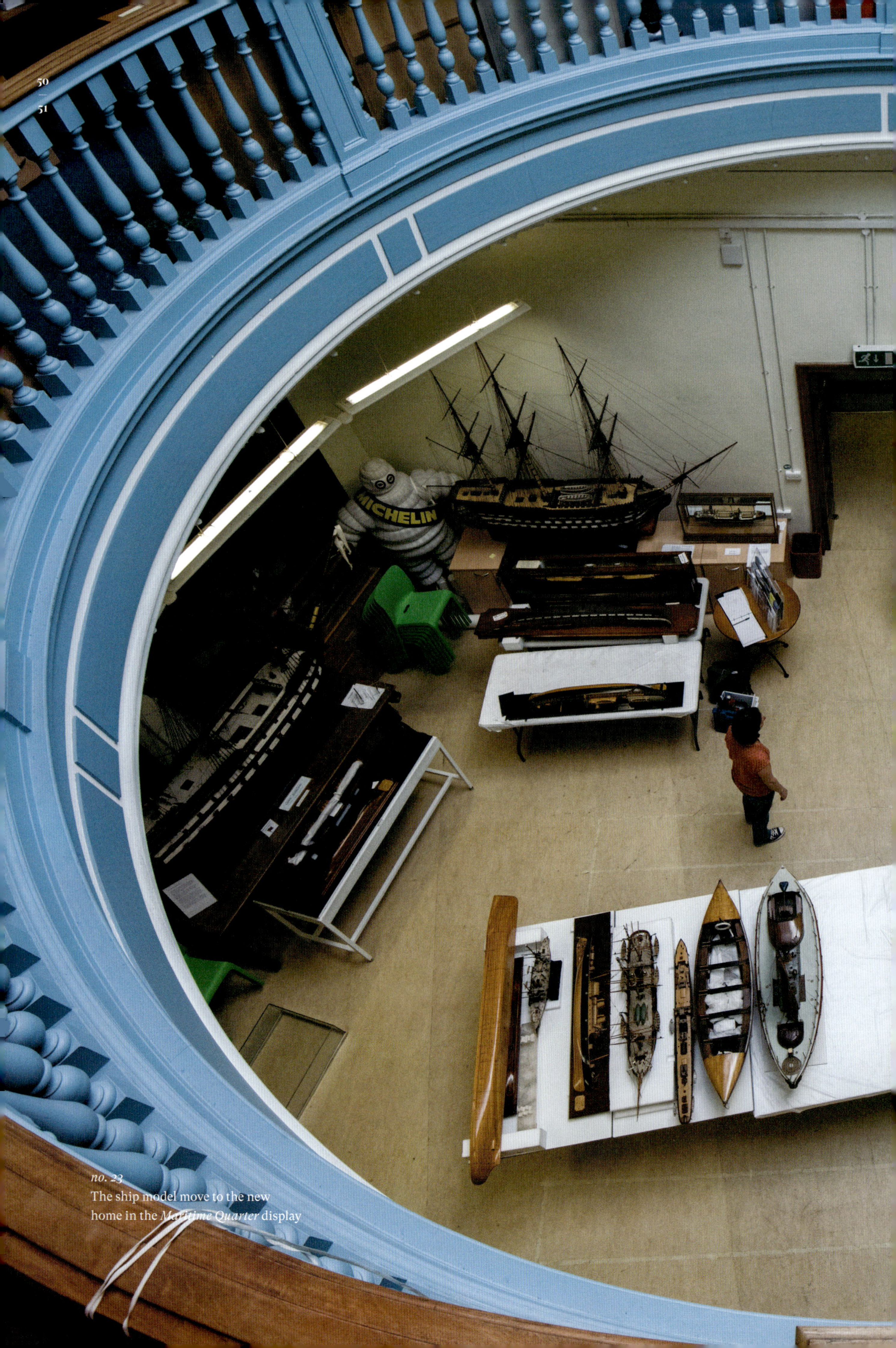

no. 23
The ship model move to the new home in the *Maritime Quarter* display

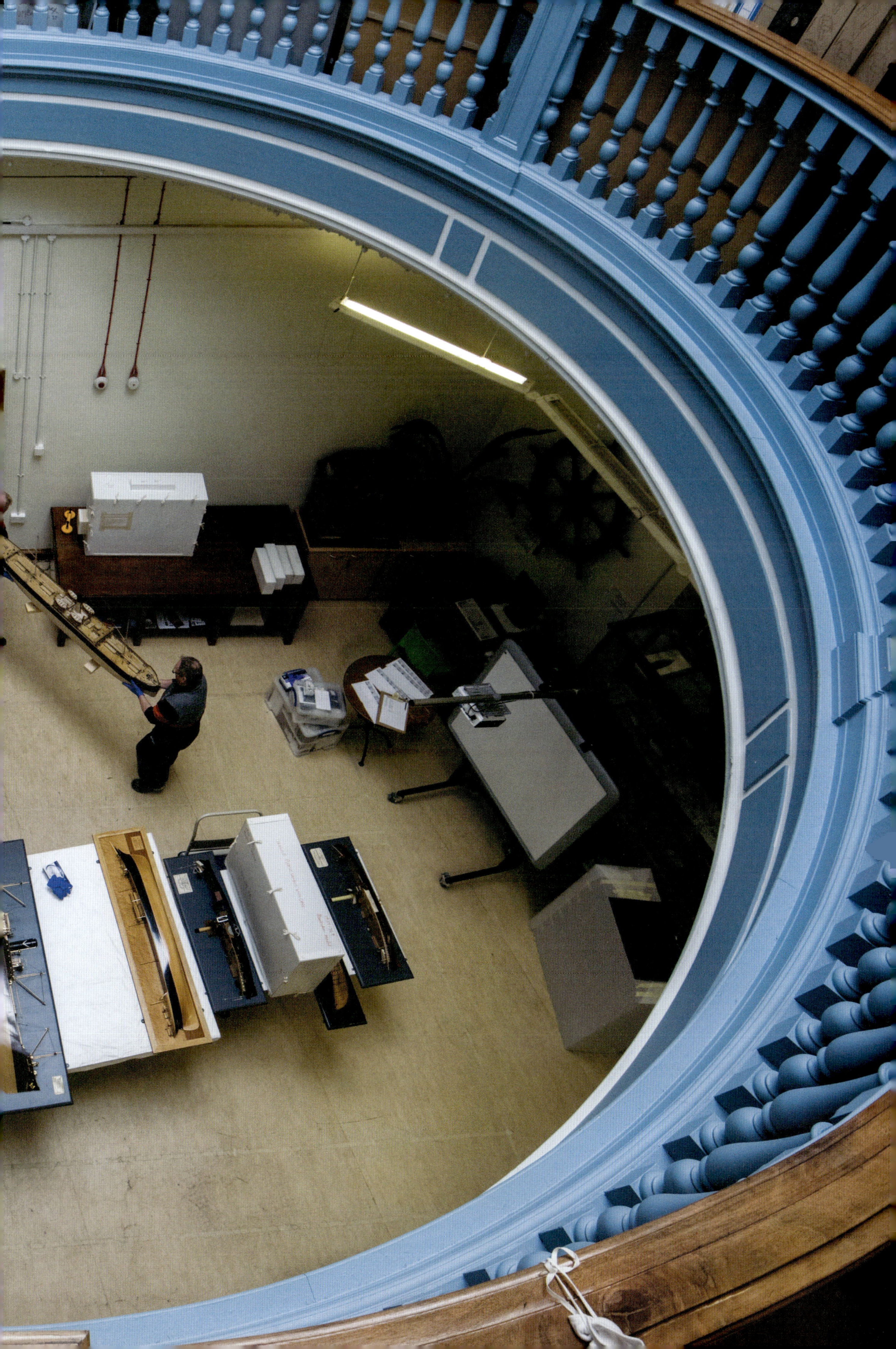

John Alexander

Leader of Dundee City Council

The Tay Whale, 1883

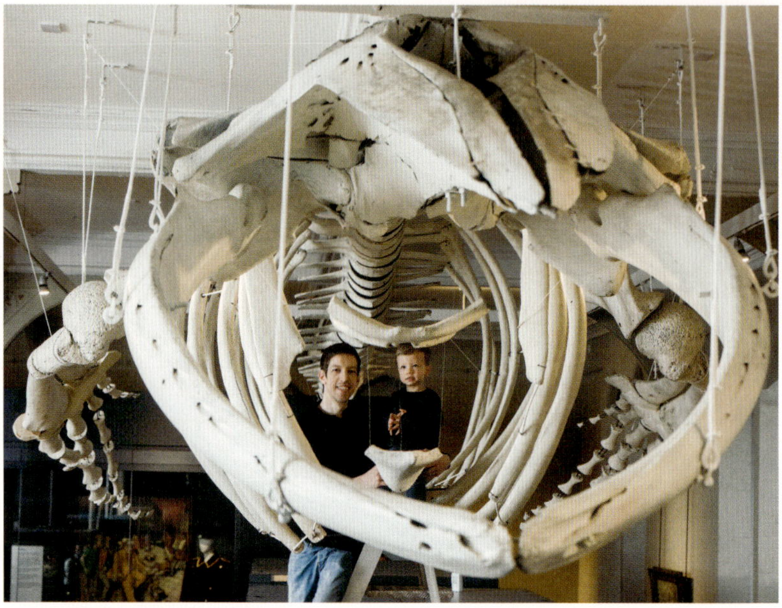

The look of excitement and joy on his wee face was phenomenal so it's a happy family memory for us.

My son, Jack, is two years old and loves everything to do with dinosaurs and animals. We came to The McManus recently as a family and when we walked in the door, Jack looked up and saw the whale bones hanging above him and shouted 'Whoah, dinosaur!'. He wasn't completely correct, of course, but the look of excitement and joy on his wee face was phenomenal so it's a happy family memory for us.

The McManus is Dundee. It's a really good reminder of what Dundee was, what Dundee is, and what it will become. It's important to remember what Dundee was built upon and relate that to what we're trying to do now.

The really special thing is the way they constantly change the exhibits so there's always something new and exciting to see. I can come here with my granny or with my son and there's something that will excite each of them. That's what The McManus is, something for everyone and that's really special.

Lucy Byatt

Director of Hospitalfield
Arbroath

Scold's Bridle

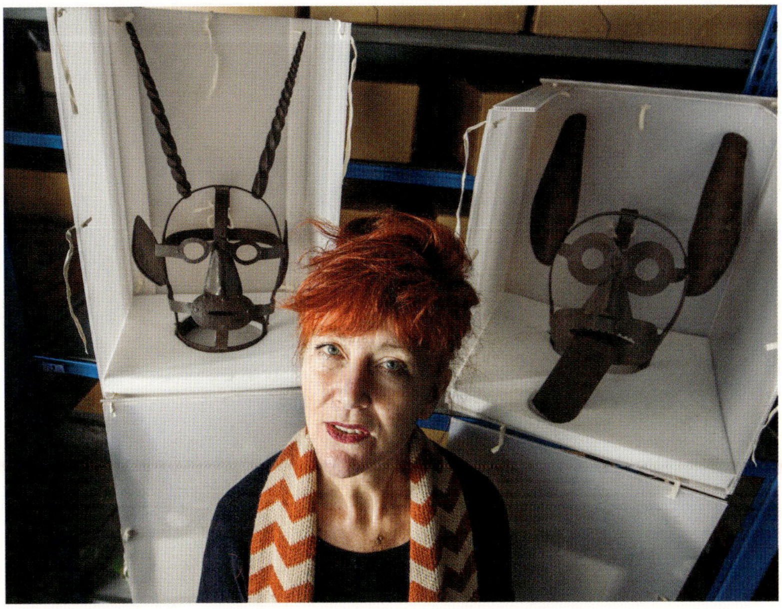

The masks always stayed in my subconscious, they drifted in and out my mind.

Attracted to Dundee through the strength of the public art debate, in 1990 I accepted the offer of an artist's residency at Strathmartine Hospital. During these two years living in the city I visited The McManus often and these 'scold's bridles' were memorable and extraordinary. As a form of punishment for women who spoke out they are clearly utterly cruel. The physicality of the objects and the way they are constructed makes it possible to feel the shock of their restriction; their shape and size, the rigidity of the steel bands, the flat piece of metal fitting in to the mouth to flatten the tongue.

Freedom of speech is no. 19 in the Declaration of Human Rights and is a value that I'm sure we all believe in. However, it remains a continuously contested issue and we see systems that are far crueller and more insidious than the use of these medieval cages.

With the marking of thirty years since the Clause 28 debacle I'm reminded of the culture of demonstrations of that period. The back routes that the police would send us on, the frustration of not being heard. The slow narrative emerging doggedly from the Six o'clock news. How things have changed, particularly in relation to the gushing, whooshing flow of information today. Social media makes it easier to find out what is going on but has also become an outstandingly effective mechanism for intimidation and gagging.

It shows, I think, how an object in The McManus can be a part of history but can also be part of our current and future debates.

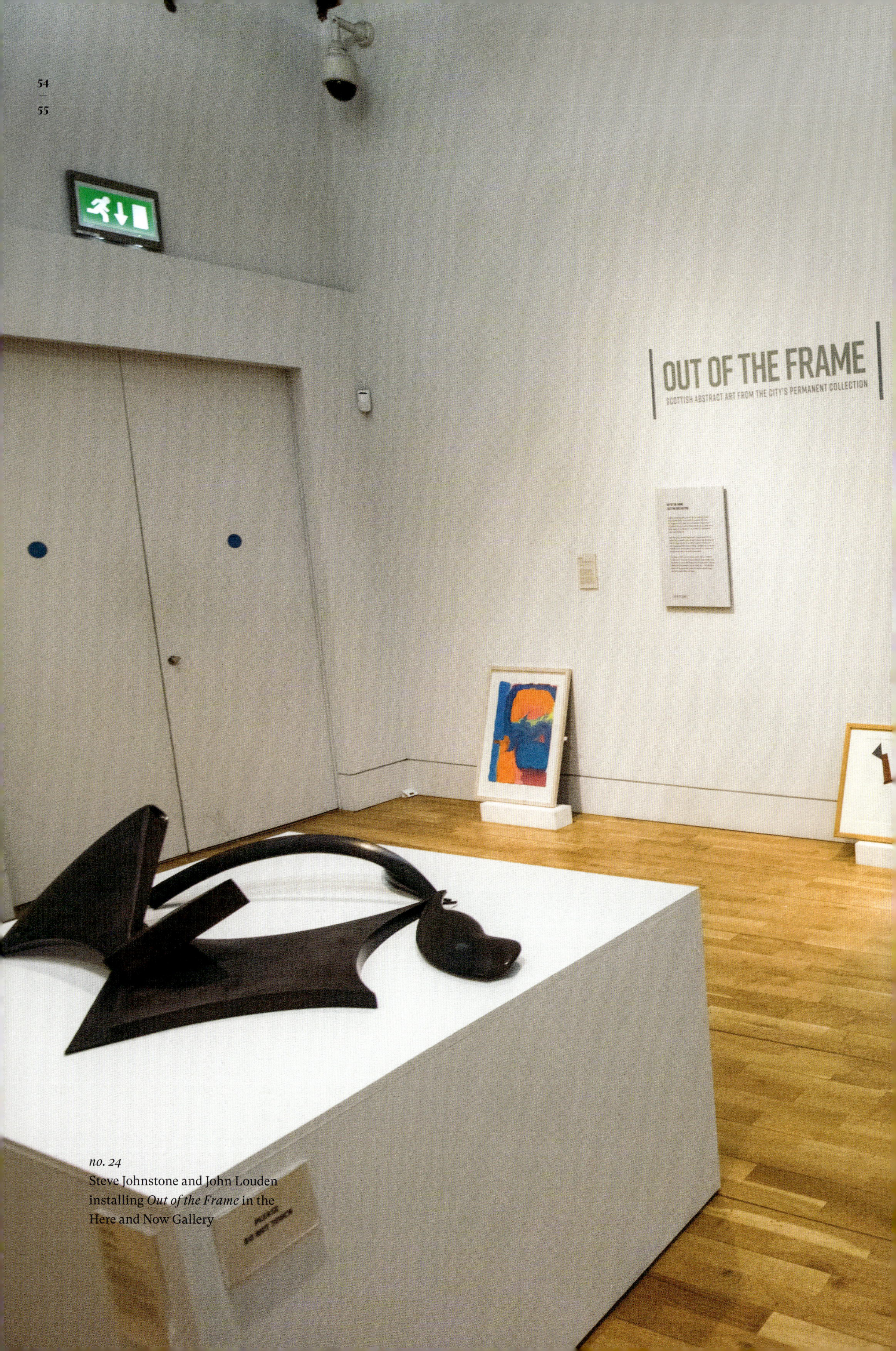

no. 24
Steve Johnstone and John Louden installing *Out of the Frame* in the Here and Now Gallery

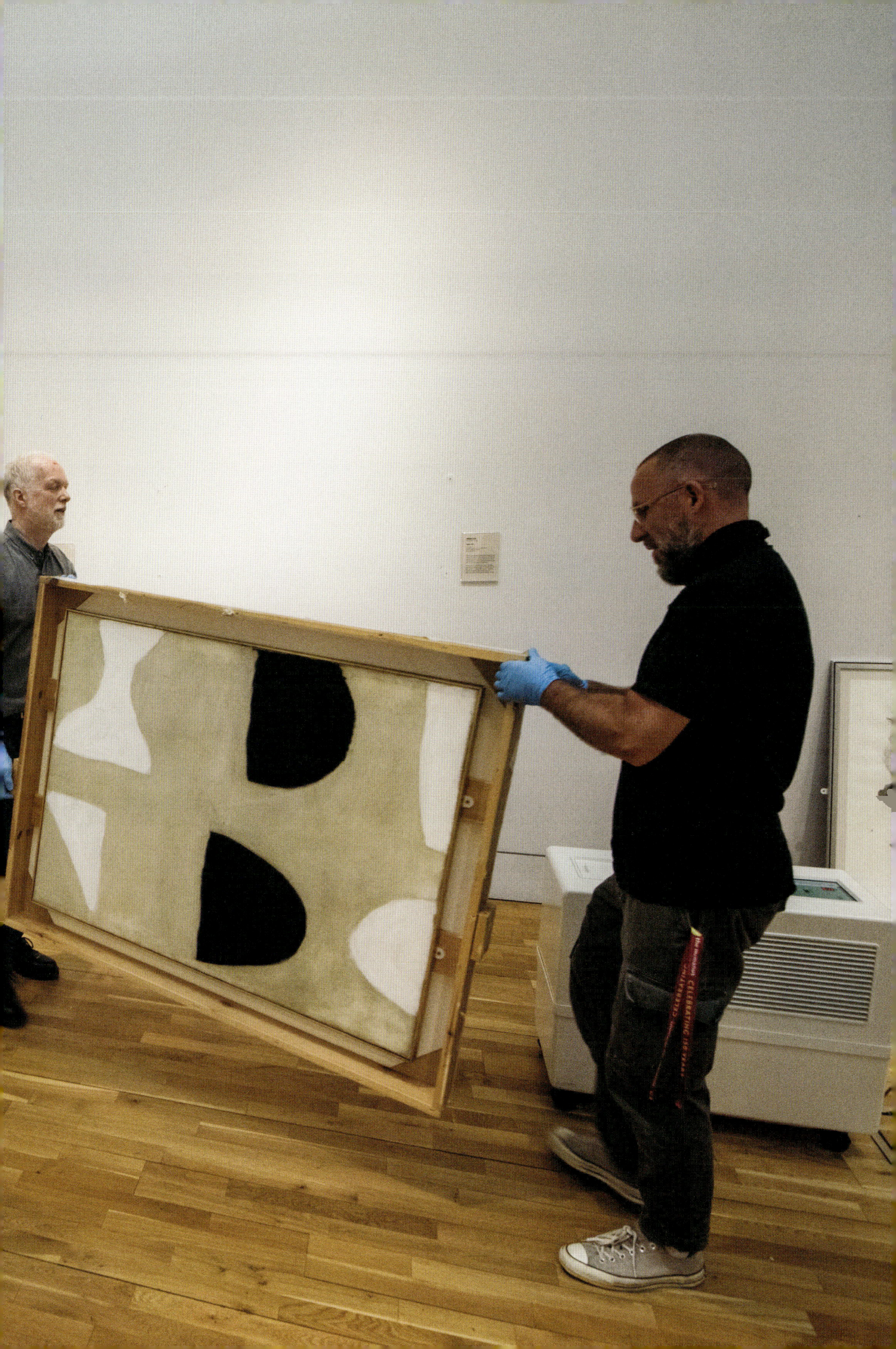

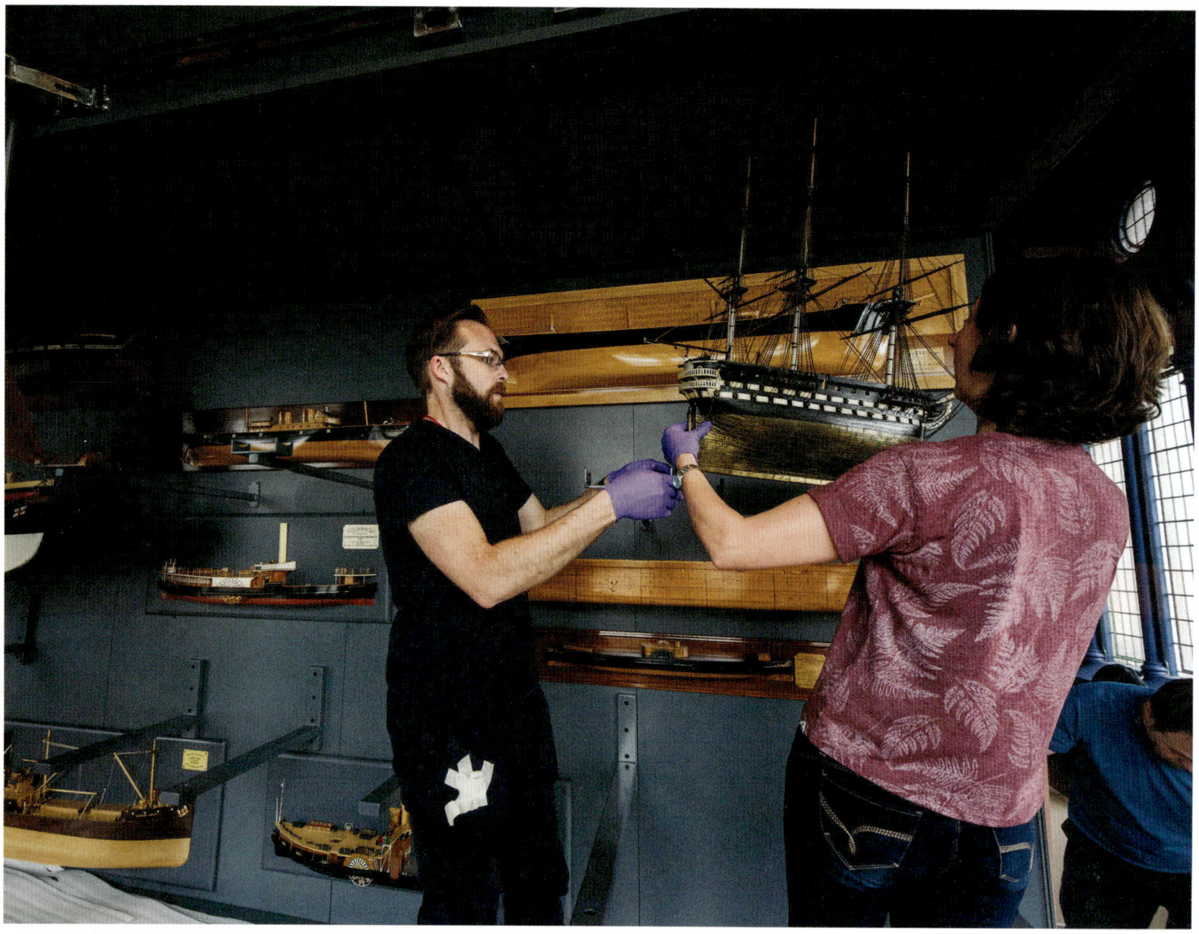

no. 25
Gareth Jackson-Hunt and Rebecca Jackson-Hunt installing ship models into the new bespoke case in the *Maritime Quarter*

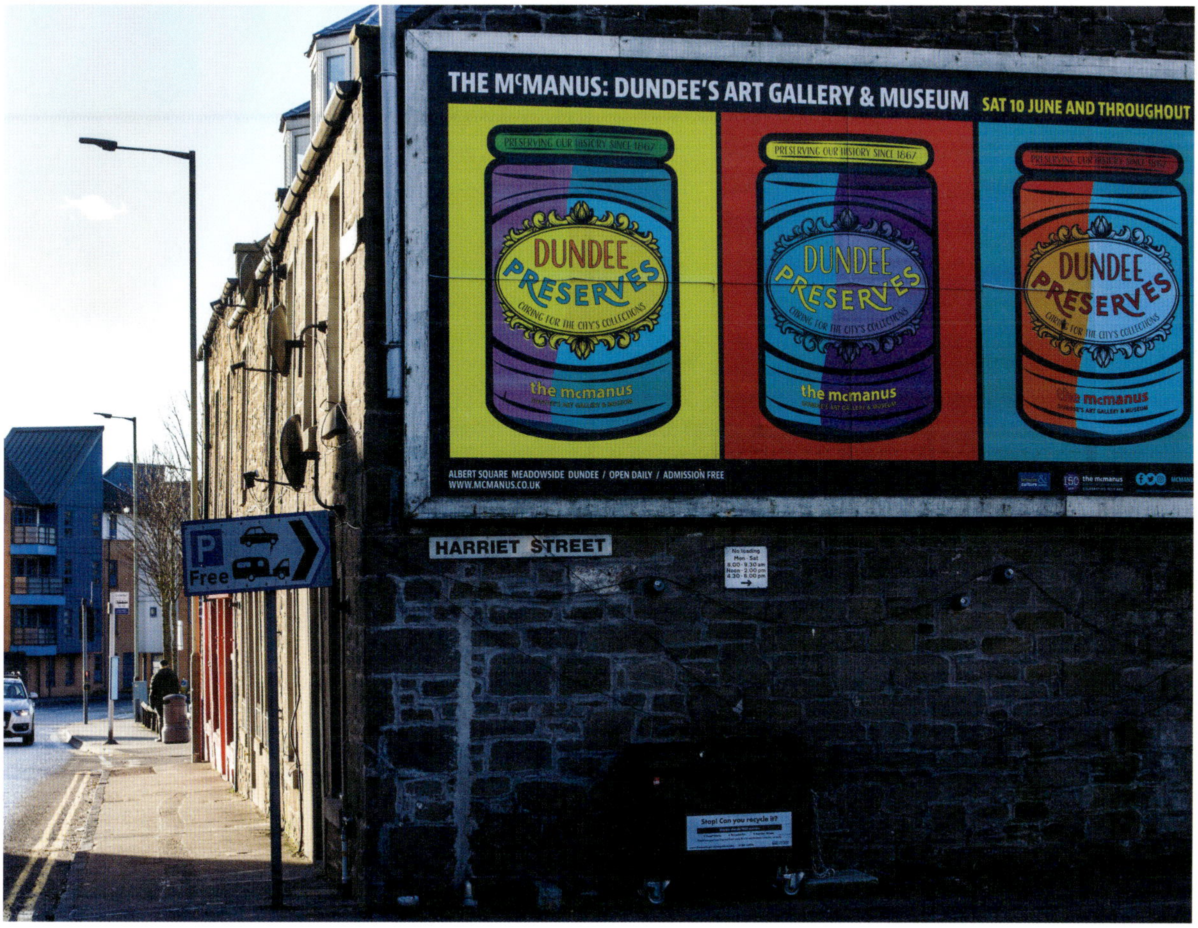

no. 26
Billboard of *Dundee Preserves: Caring for the City's Collection*, playfully referencing Dundee's marmalade making heritage

Andrew Jeffrey

Maritime Historian

The Maritime Quarter

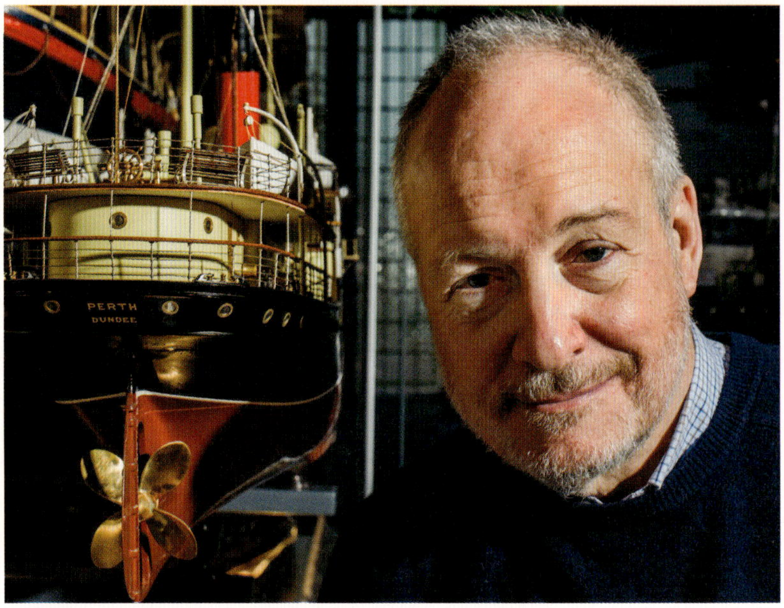

The models are made by professionals and amateurs, each has its own amazing story.

Some made by professionals, others by amateurs, the models in The McManus collection each have their own amazing story to tell. There is, for example, a fine model of the lifeboat Mona, famously lost along with her eight crew on a storm-lashed rescue mission in 1959.

Then there are models of ships that deserve to be better known. The DP&L coaster Perth, launched from Dundee's Caledon Shipyard in 1915, was requisitioned by the Royal Navy, fitted with guns and sailed for the Red Sea. In June 1916 she took part in the bombardment of Jeddah, forcing the surrender of the Turkish garrison, an event that marked the start of the Arab revolt.

Badly damaged in a battle with a U-Boat which left two of her crew dead, Perth was returned to her owners, but was called up again in the Second World War, eventually saving the lives of 455 Allied seamen and airmen.

On a lighter note, there is a fine model of the Tay Ferries paddle steamer Forfarshire, launched in 1864. A popular Tay excursion steamer with a busy licensed bar, Forfarshire's arrival with a cargo of inebriated passengers would strike fear into the residents of Newburgh. Often the steamer would simply sail away and leave drunken passengers lying about the village.

Yet Maritime Quarter at The McManus is more than just a collection of ship models; it is a remarkable record of Dundee as one of Scotland's great sea ports, of the men and women who built the ships, the passengers who trod their decks and the crews who sailed them to the far corners of the world.

Calum Colvin

Artist and Lecturer, Duncan of Jordanstone College of Art and Design, University of Dundee.

Jacobite Flag

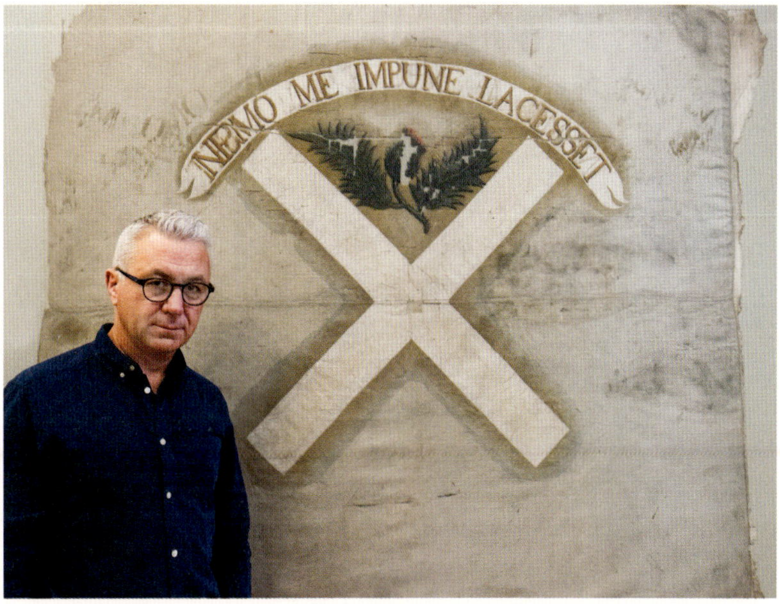

I noticed that there was a great deal of affection for The McManus, especially the gallery.

My memories of The McManus stretch back to when I first came to Dundee as a student at Duncan of Jordanstone College of Art and Design in 1979. At that point, Dundee was a little down at heel, suffering particularly in the general economic decline. There were lots of derelict buildings around and The McManus' Gothic splendour was looking a little faded, certainly when we compare it to its current reincarnation!

Of course, as a young art student with a passion for photography that aesthetic of urban decay in itself was interesting to me and inspired many photographic expeditions under the tutelage of the great Joe McKenzie. As I got to know my new Dundonian friends, it was interesting to get their view on the city, and I noticed that there was a great deal of affection for The McManus, especially the gallery (now called Landscapes and Lives I) which houses the natural history exhibits. This struck a chord with me, reminiscent of my own childhood fascination with museum culture and its effect on the youthful imagination: our first close up view of the natural world, of the history of cities, of the wonders of engineering are often shaped by these institutions! This is especially true with The McManus, which connects so wonderfully with the history and culture of Dundee.

The object I chose to be pictured with is the famous Jacobite flag of the Angus regiment under Lord Ogilvy. One of only two surviving Jacobite flags, it was reputedly carried onto Culloden battlefield in 1746. Beautiful and delicate, I was taken with its fragility, its poignancy and its historical resonance.

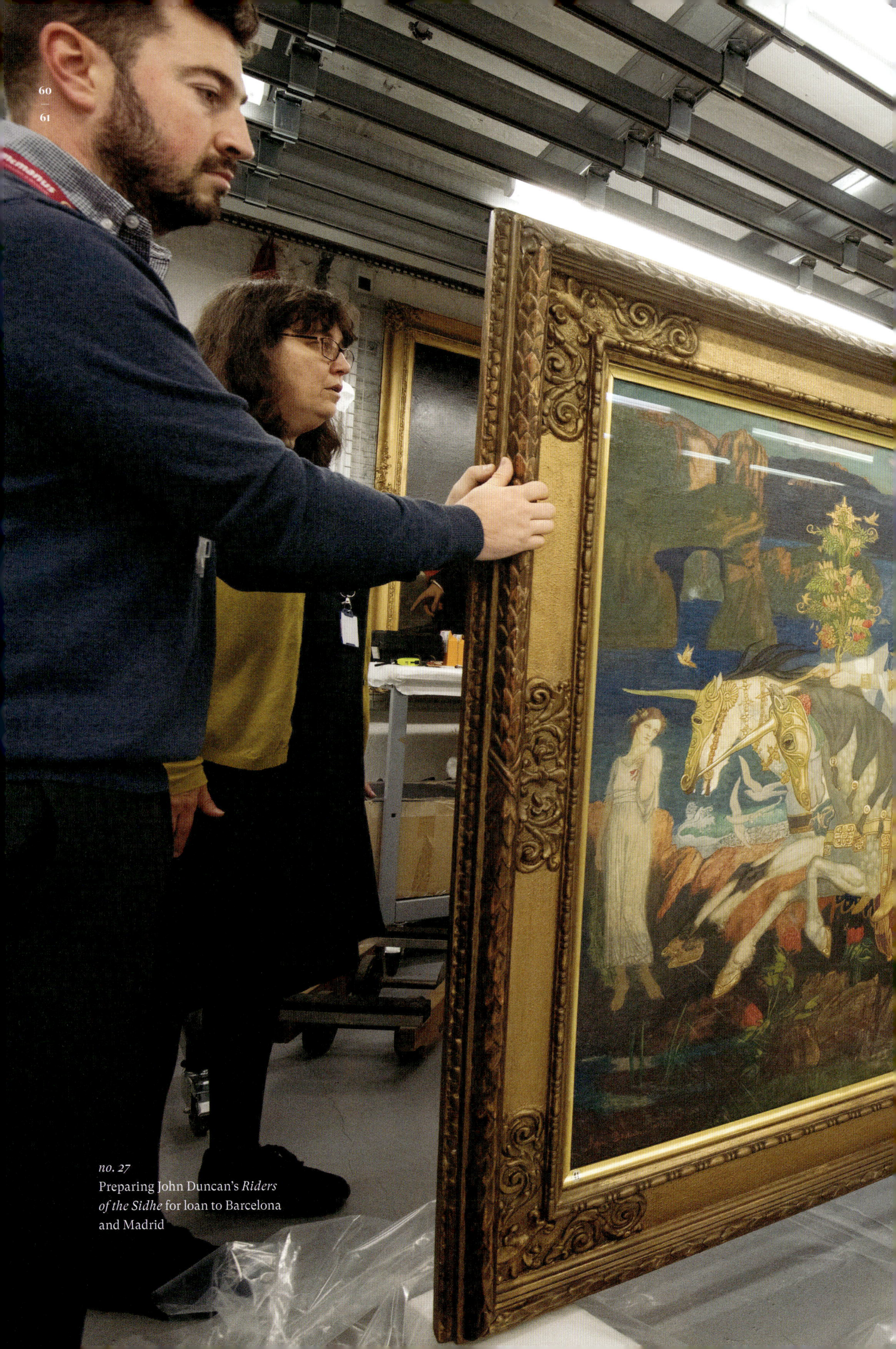

no. 27
Preparing John Duncan's *Riders of the Sidhe* for loan to Barcelona and Madrid

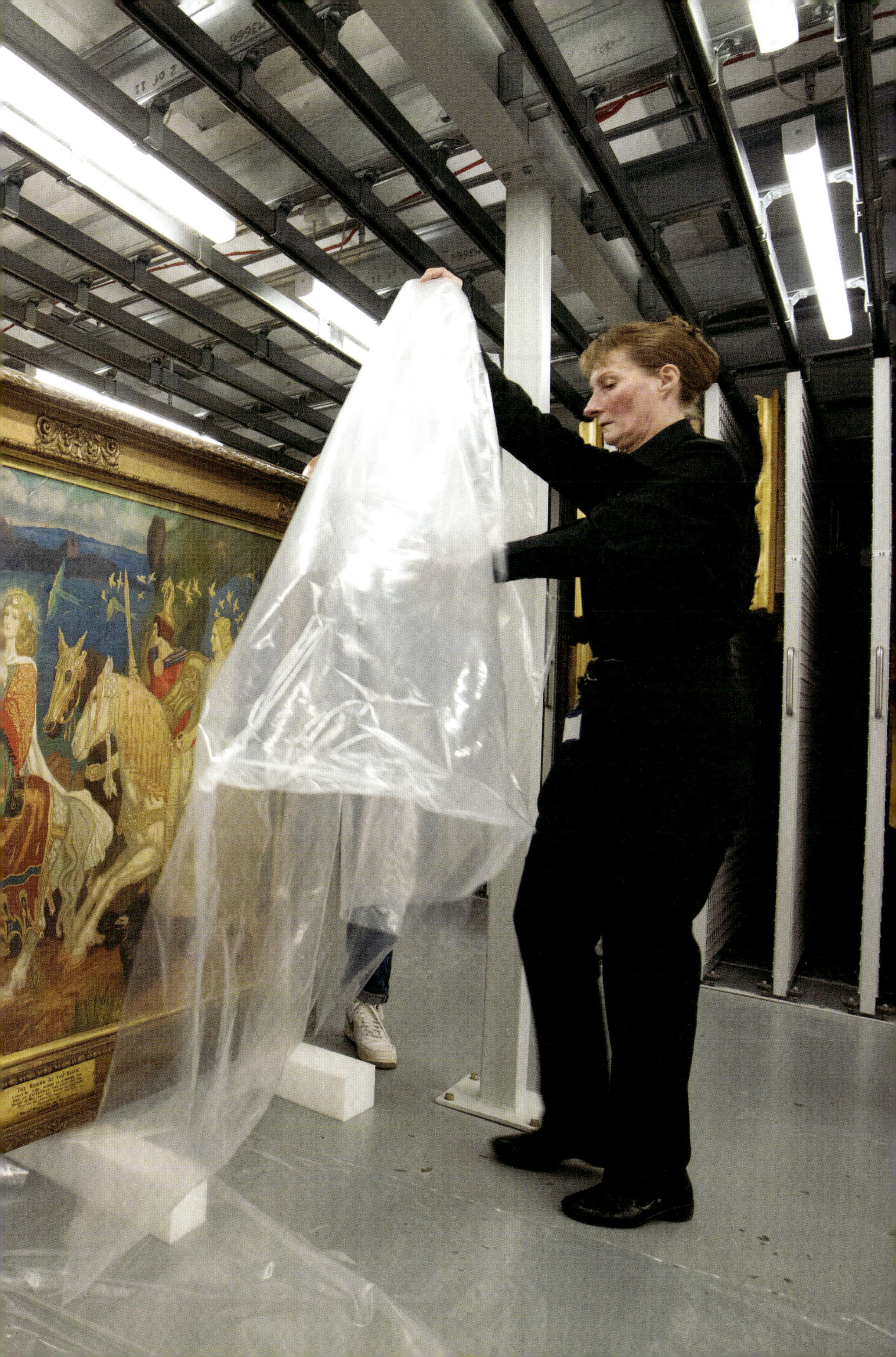
"THE RIDERS OF THE SIDHE"

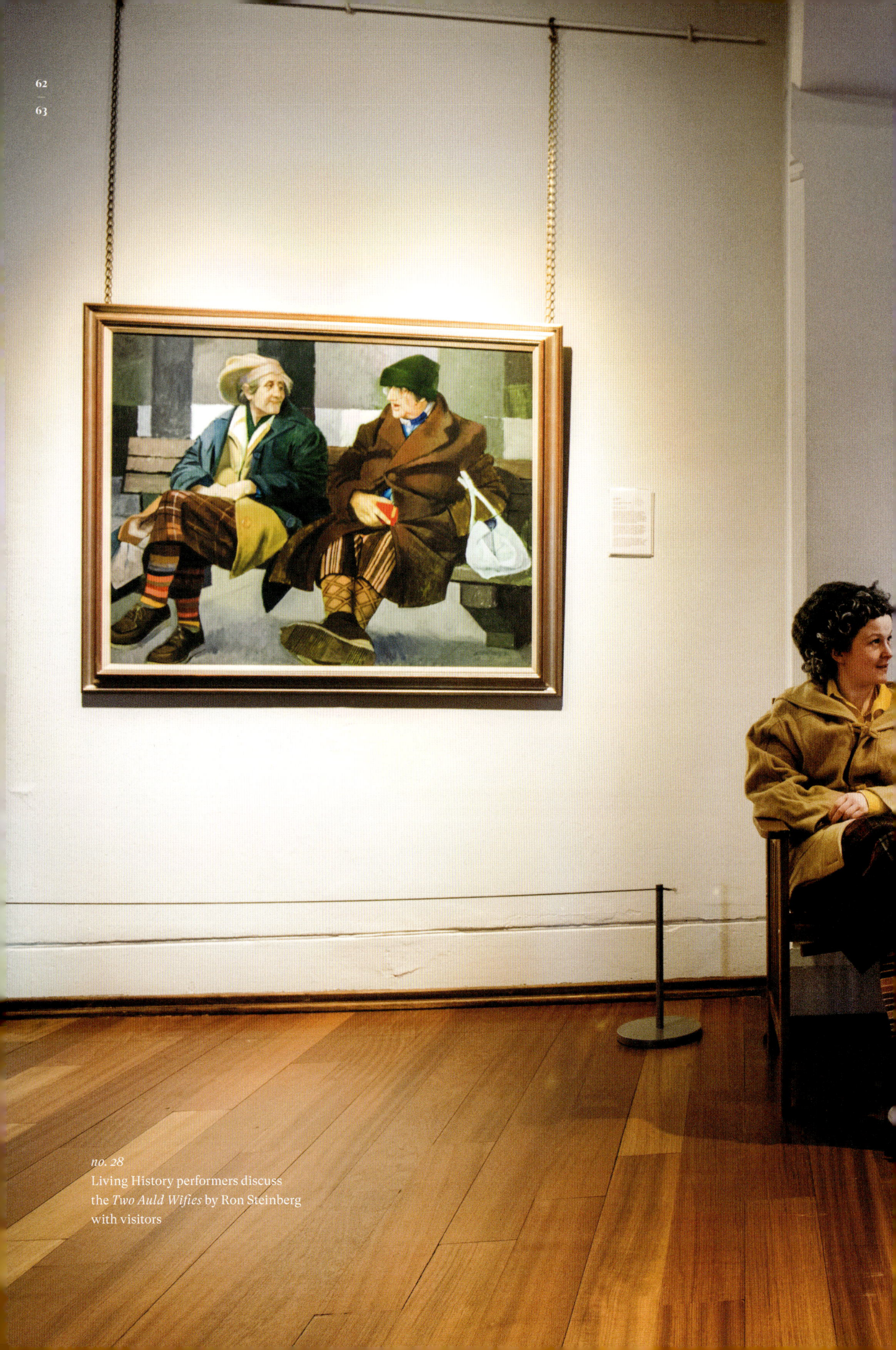

no. 28
Living History performers discuss the *Two Auld Wifies* by Ron Steinberg with visitors

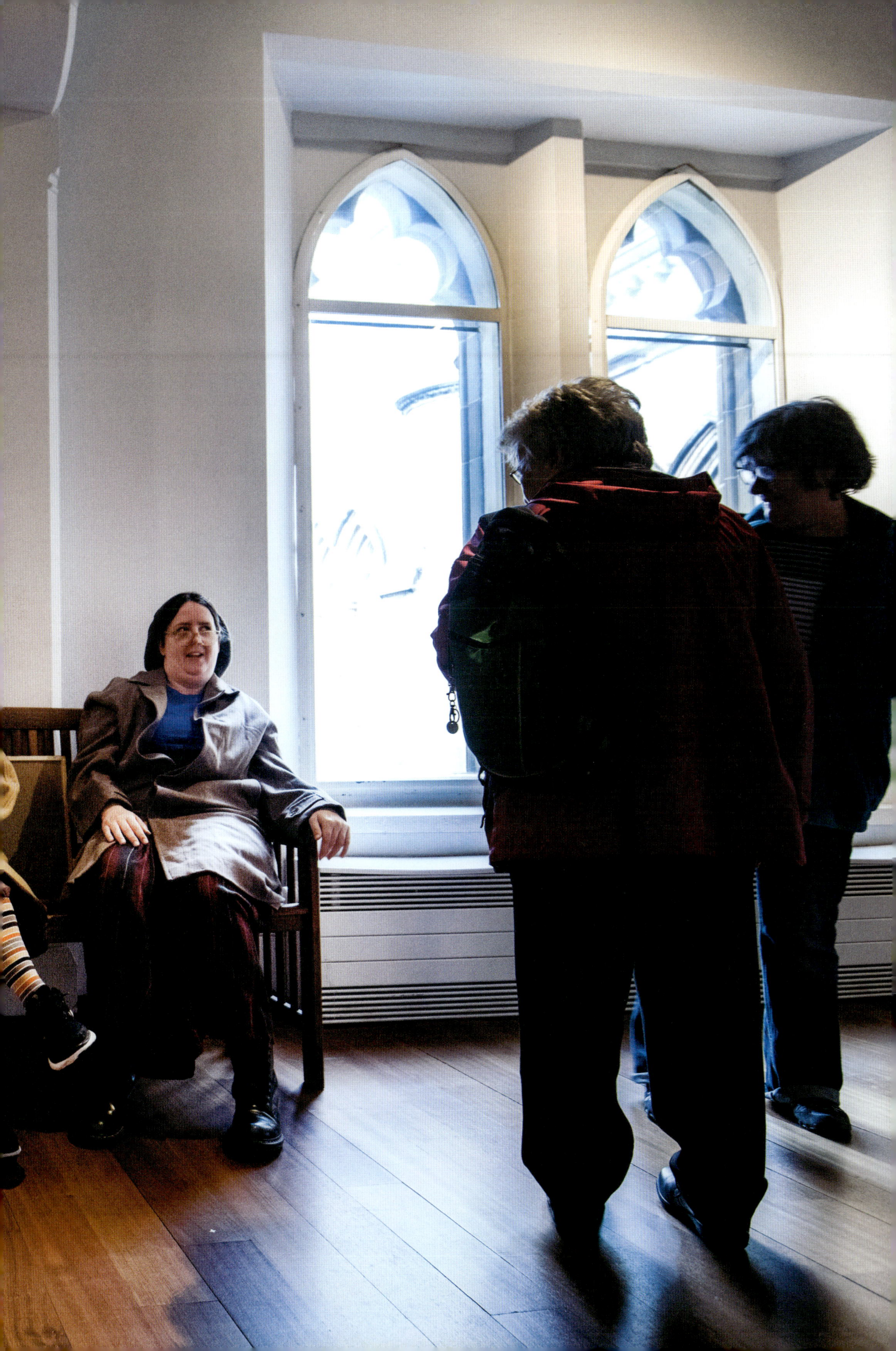

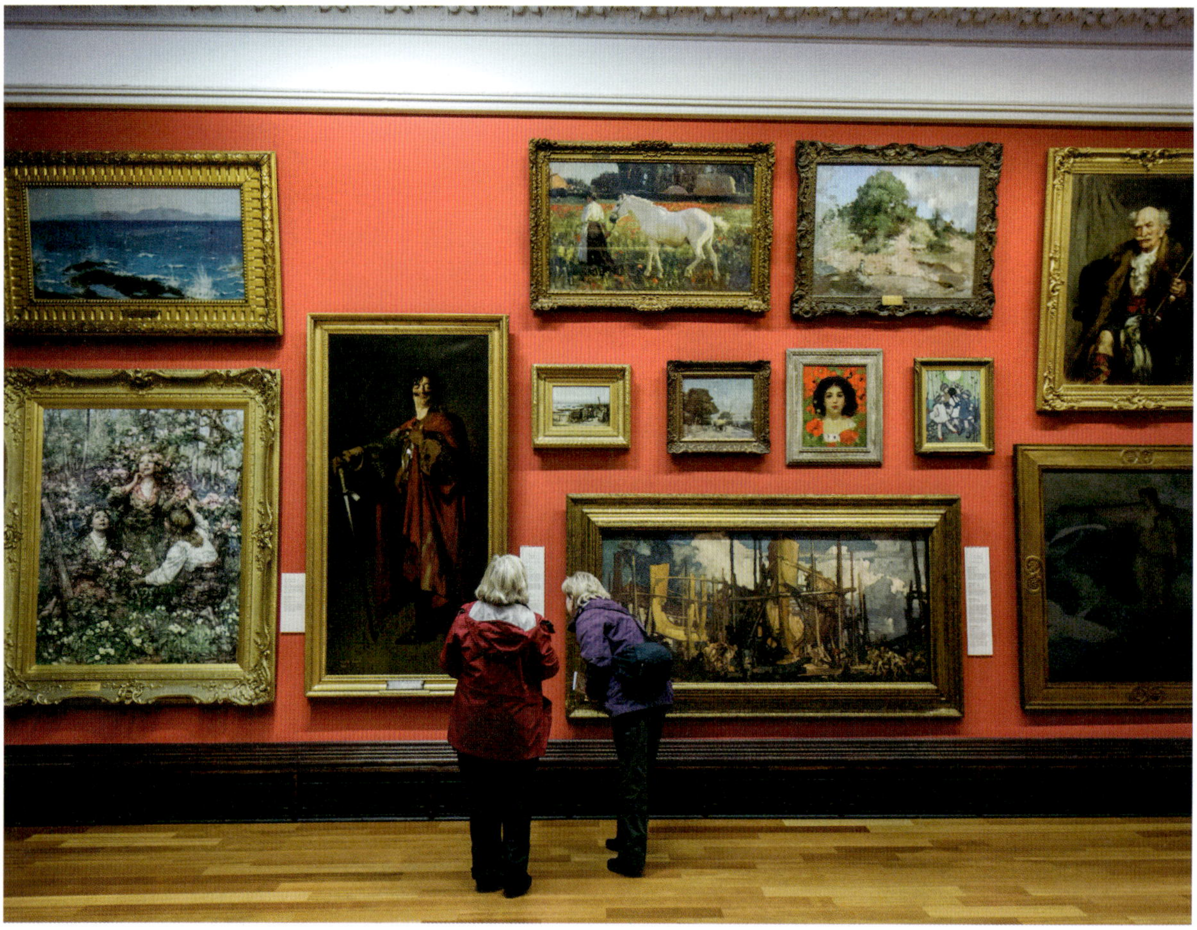

no. 29
Visitors in the museum's
Victoria Gallery

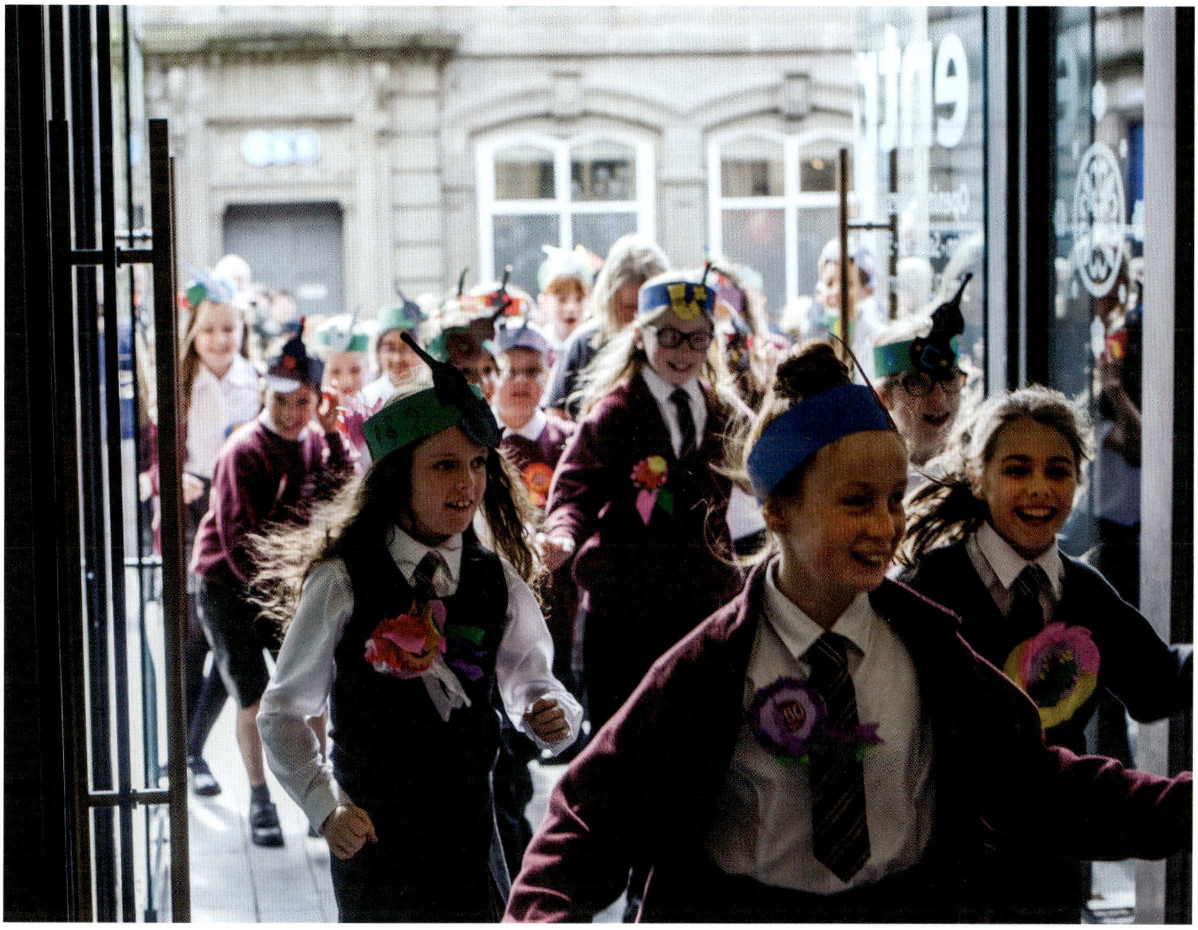

no. 30
Enthusiastic schoolchildren
at the 150th anniversary event
at The McManus

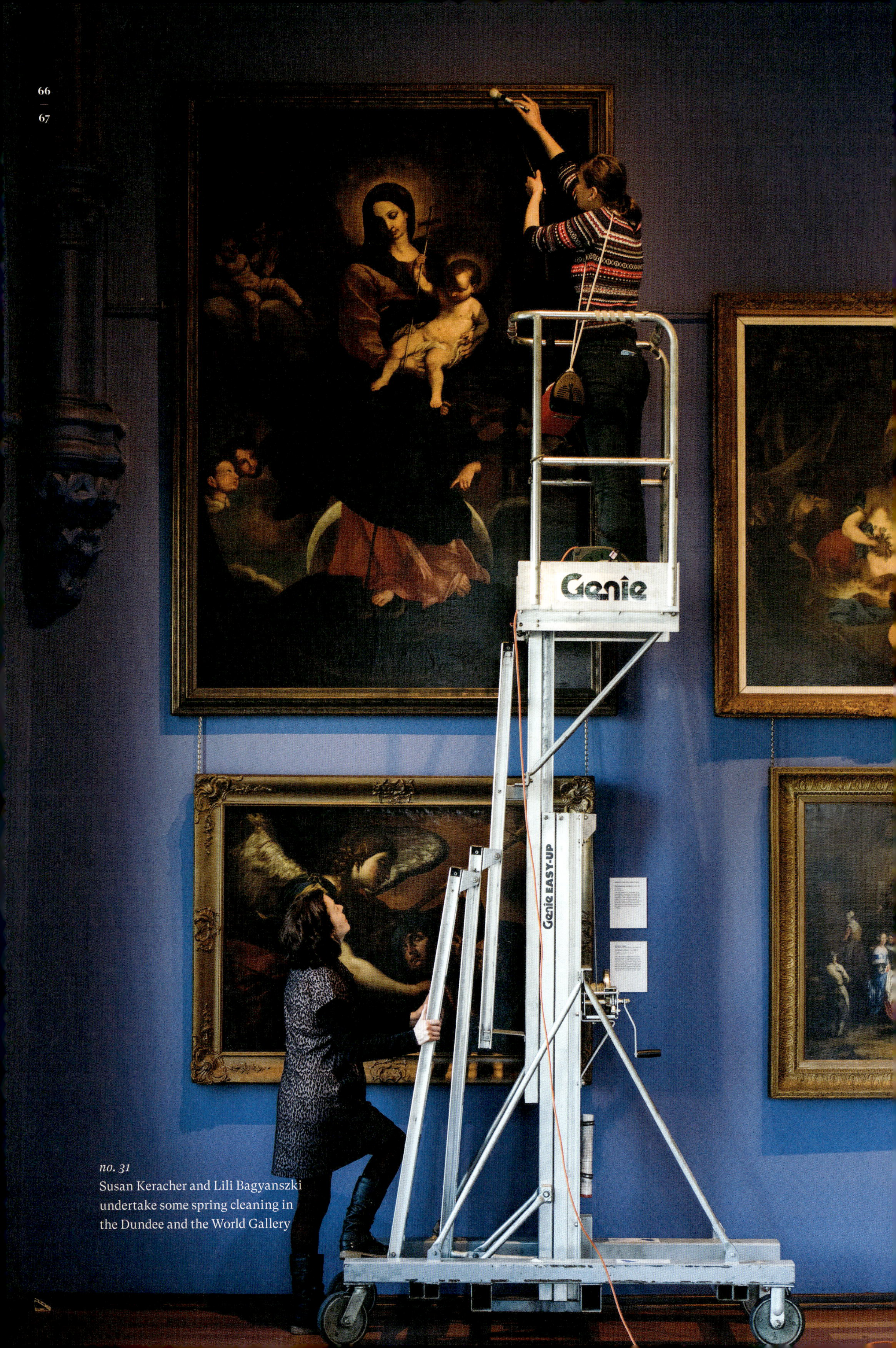

no. 31
Susan Keracher and Lili Bagyanszki undertake some spring cleaning in the Dundee and the World Gallery

Douglas Beer

Visitor Assistant

War Club c.1850-96
North American, Great Lakes,
Chippewa people

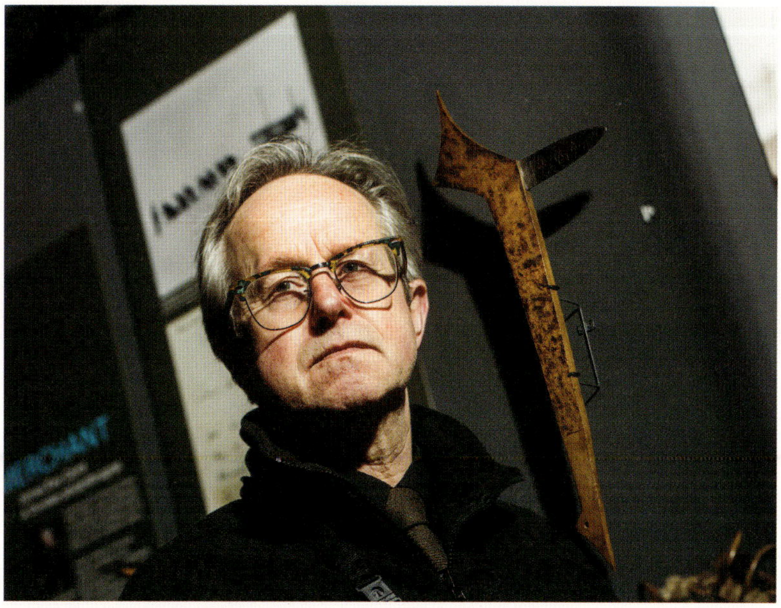

The object I picked is one I remember from my youth, a Chippewa war club...It's a killing tool.

The object I picked is one I remember from my youth, a Chippewa war club; or, in other words, a battle axe owned by a Native American. It's a killing tool. If the metal bit went into your head, you're not going anywhere. But if you look carefully you'll see that it's actually been a 21-inch steel rule. So the question I asked myself was, how did the Native American find it – did he steal it, did he trade for it?

The story is long gone, we'll never know now.

The shaft of the battle axe is made out of a rifle butt. So he's taken two killing tools and recreated them into his own, with poker work at the top and a sacred fire bird down the side. It's a lovely, powerful thing.

As a young guy, if I'd been to the swimming, or down to the arcade, me and my friends would come in and we'd maybe cause a bit of a riot. It was my sticky fingers, my nose up against the glass. That was me. This item just captured my imagination, it made me think of lone rangers and cowboys. I'm from Dundee and have been coming here all my life. This place gave me a real love for museums. I'm enthusiastic like nobody else about this place. The variety is so special, it's a traditional people's museum.

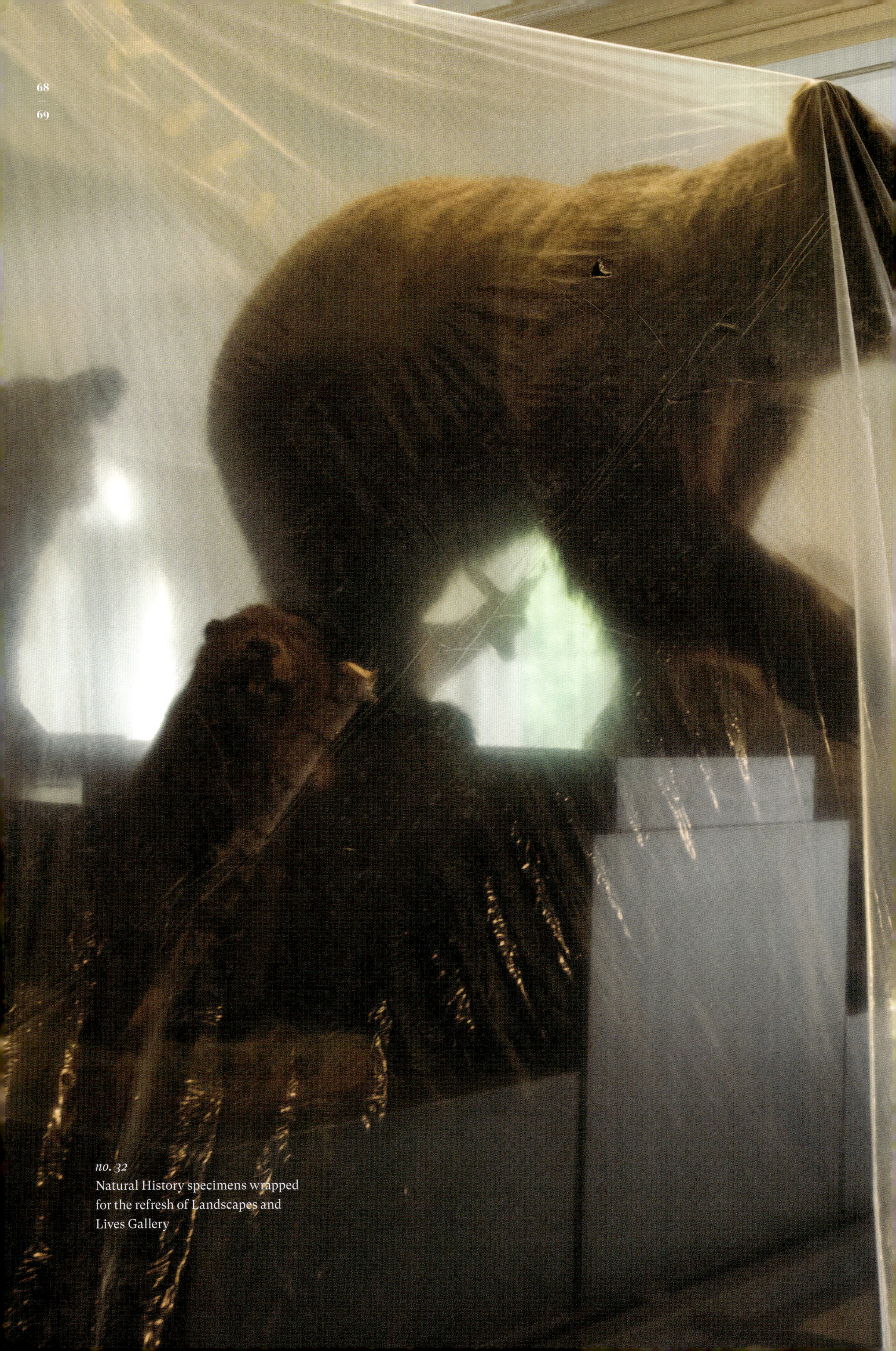

no. 32
Natural History specimens wrapped for the refresh of Landscapes and Lives Gallery

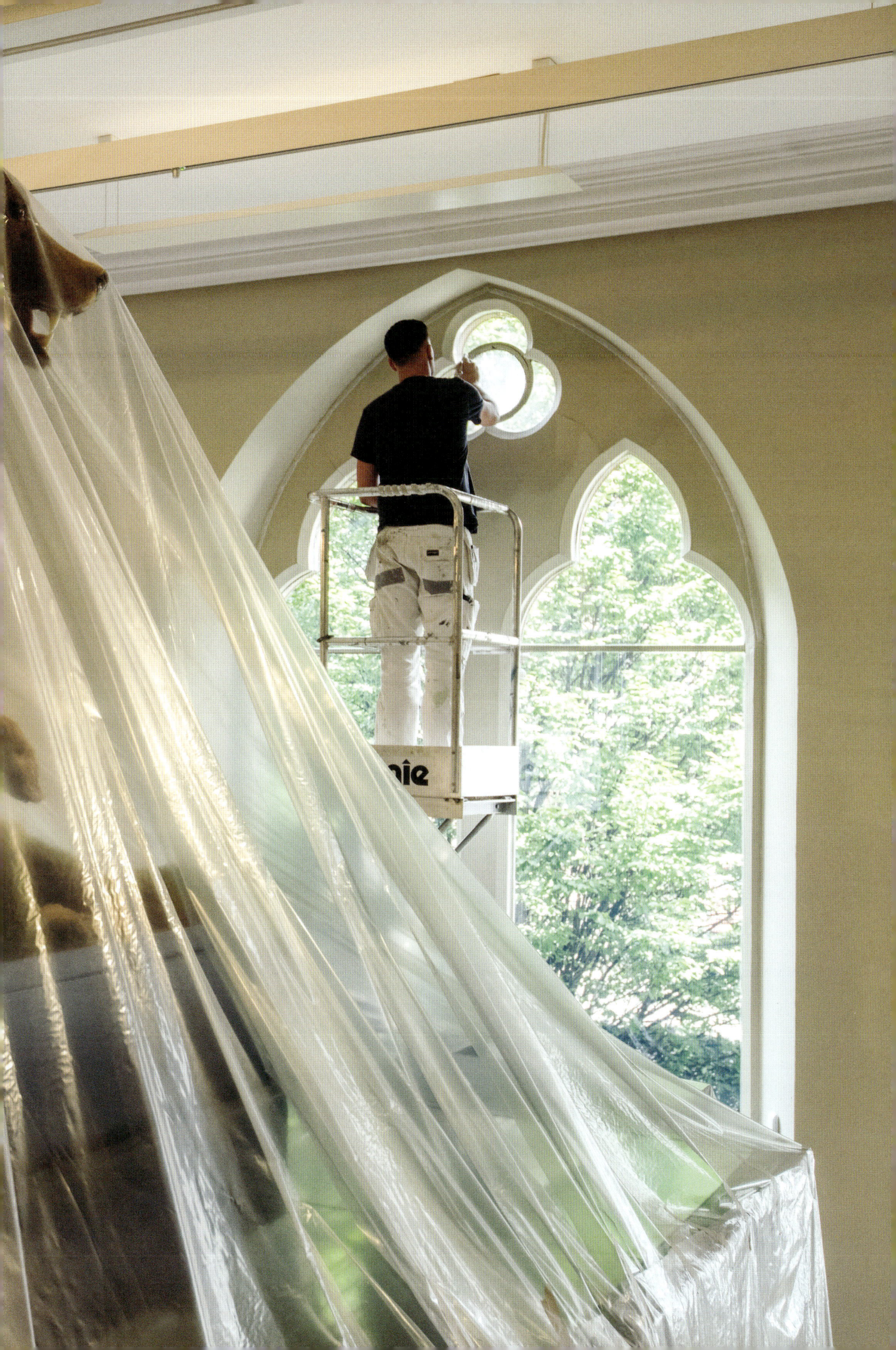

Kirstie Skinner

Director, Outset Scotland

Girls and Horses, Hacienda Tucle, Huancayo, 2013, Corin Sworn

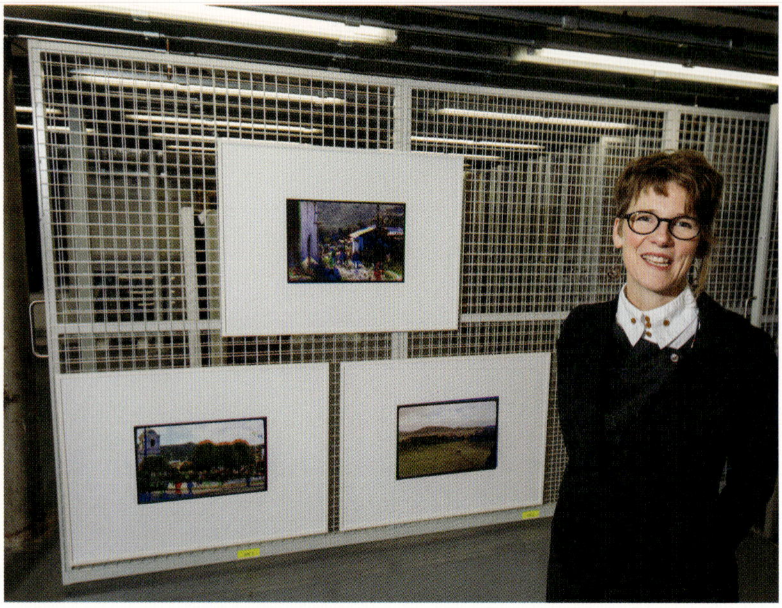

I was drawn to the way the artist interweaved her own memories with her father's experiences.

My chosen works are by Corin Sworn. The suite was the first gift my organisation, Outset Scotland, made to a public collection. I was drawn to the way the artist interweaved her own memories with her father's experiences as a social anthropologist, and excited that the works might complement and comment on The McManus collections. The McManus holds an impressive array of artefacts amassed by explorers, missionaries, merchant adventurers and the like, and the contemporary art curators have sought out the same spirit in artists – people who are venturing out into the world, exploring our reality and our environment, and bringing their ideas back to the gallery.

Sworn's starting point was a recently rediscovered collection of slides taken by her father during his fieldwork in a Peruvian village in the 1970s. They travelled back to Peru together to visit the community he'd lived with. Crucially, she brought the photographs with her, and they proved to be a great talking point, which features in the video work. She also re-photographed some of her father's landscape images. Using colour separations, Sworn then superimposed three time states – the original, and two contemporary images, taken five minutes apart – creating these haunted images.

I hope they prompt visitors to think about what it is to collect images from past times, from cultures that are geographically remote from this one, and to reflect on how they themselves create and retrieve their memories.

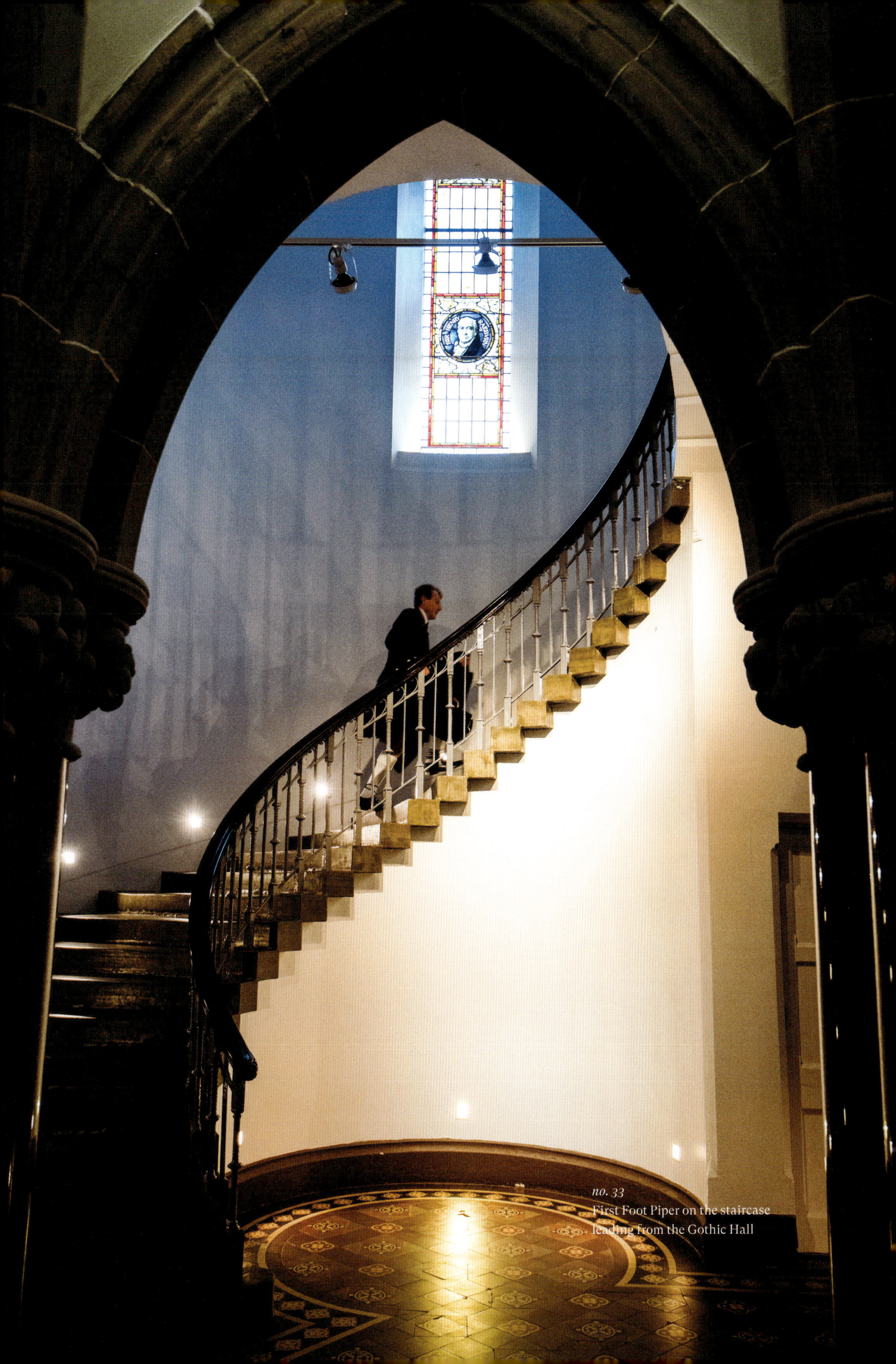

no. 33
First Foot Piper on the staircase leading from the Gothic Hall

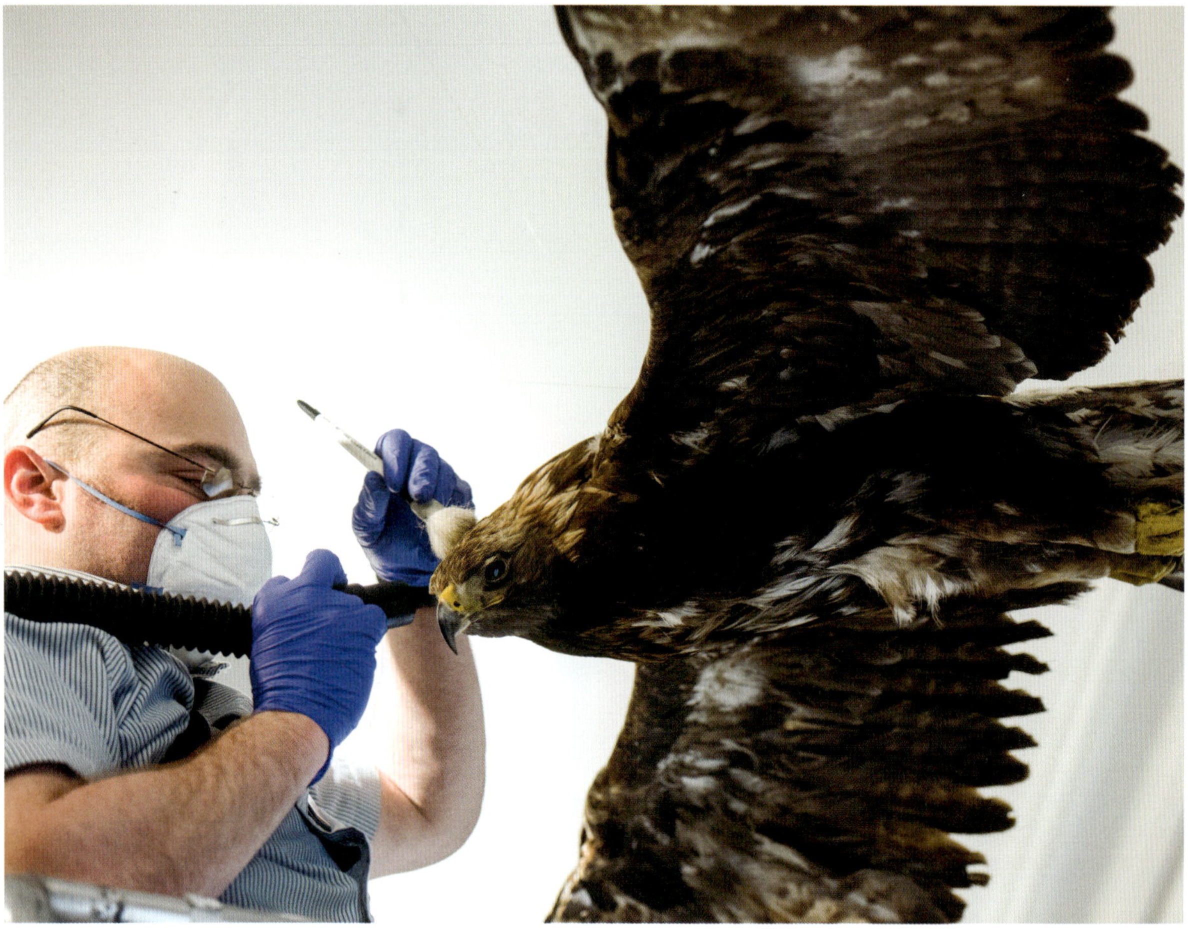

no. 34
Michael Sedakat carefully cleaning the Golden Eagle as part of our annual spring clean

Iain Flett

Retired Archivist

Portrait of James Scott Skinner – The Strathspey King, 1913, John Young Hunter

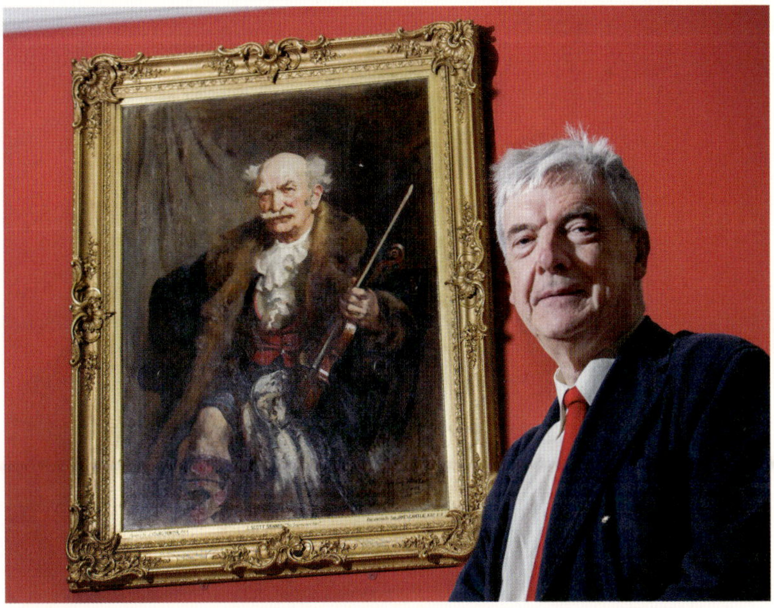

Scott Skinner is marmite to Scottish fiddlers who either love or hate him. I love him, obviously.

My chosen picture is the Strathspey King, James Scott Skinner from Banffshire. Scott Skinner is marmite to Scottish fiddlers who either love or hate him. I love him, obviously. The traditionalists say that he didn't do any favours to the traditional music but I think he took it to another level. He was a great showman. All you have to do is look at his kilt, the Harry Lauder outfit with the lace, the wonderful hair. He would challenge people to something akin to a boxing match. You could try and play faster reels that Scott Skinner, but he would always face you down. My favourite is the *Bonnie Lass of Bon Accord*, where he takes the original theme and creates two wonderful variations on top of it, making it a concert piece.

Fiddle has always been a big part of my life. My wife is a fiddle teacher, I'm a fiddle player. I love the new Sistema project in Dundee. Scottish children should have a music education.

I'm retired now, but I was the city archivist for forty years and when I came to Dundee, the reference library and the fantastic collection of Lamb images was crammed into this building. I know my colleagues had a huge problem with green mould in the basement. Now it's a beautiful building to just be in, to take time out and to enjoy the splendour.

The Com

munities

The Communities

People make the museum. The belief that the public are there to interact with the objects, to learn from the museum and teach it too – that's why The McManus has remained at the heart of Dundee for 150 years. It was built with the strong belief that if you have a well-informed and vibrant community, it makes the city a better place to live.

The Albert Institute – the original name for The McManus – was built by public subscription, as a way of honouring the late Prince Albert. Although most of the build, which was to contain a library, a reading room for ladies and a facility for lectures and concerts, was paid for by prosperous jute mill owners, ordinary Dundonians also put their money towards the fine new centre for learning.

It was created not as a depository for beautiful and interesting objects, but it was meant to be energised and used by people for well-being and learning. From the start, the position of the museum, in the centre of the city, has meant that it remains a hub for people to meet and be inspired, to connect with the place and the objects.

The McManus 168 Supporters group have spent the last year researching the people who paid for the building, so their stories can be told. Named after the number of 'subscribers' that were originally thought to have been part of the proper gang, the project has uncovered that there was actually 327.

Sue Moody, chair of the McManus 168 Supporters, has been part of the team uncovering the stories of the people who made the institution.

"The project to uncover the stories of all the people who made the Albert Institute a reality is an exciting one. We've involved historians, archivists, family history people, genealogists and we've recruited more than 100 volunteers who don't have any experience in this kind of research. We're developing a website which will be a permanent legacy for the project. That way, people worldwide will get to know about the original subscribers. Eventually there will also be exhibitions, talks, displays, a song, and original artwork – to celebrate the Dundonians who made The McManus possible."

Today, The McManus (renamed in 1984), is home to a choir in residence who practise in and around the building, inspired by the art and the objects. When Loadsaweeminsingin' are heard – at Christmas, at New Year First Footing celebrations, at any special occasion – their melodies seem to be entirely in harmony with the fabric of the building itself. The group comprises of women who have become friends and colleagues, from all across the city.

Dads arrive with their children; school children pour through the door. Artists sketch and writers come for inspiration. The McManus is seen as a space where creativity in all its forms can blossom.

At celebratory times of the year, such as Christmas and Halloween, families from all over the region come to take part in activities from storytelling to craft, spreading out across the museum and enjoying every part of the space. Music adds to the atmosphere, encouraging new faces and more visits.

There are other moments of fun. The annual Festival of Museums is a time in the year when the museum attracts a huge crowd and the Learning and Engagement team brings together creative people from around the city – from sketchers to musicians, for an extravaganza of excitement, encouraging people to engage with the museum in a different and active way. Children come and chat with the museum staff, parents wander round the collections.

The museum has a close relationship with partners in the city, including the University of Dundee and Abertay University, who co-host a series of fascinating talks called Café Arts. Open to the public, these events are a perfect blend of interesting subjects and expert speakers and are always popular.

The museum is more than just the objects. The galleries grow with the audiences, prompting better engagement and more meaningful exchange. There are programmes to collect memories through oral histories, to ensure those stories are collected for the future.

The enjoyment felt at the museum also has the impact of serious learning. Christine Millar, Section Leader, Learning and Engagement has been a core part of The McManus team for 18 years and has helped develop the outreach approach that has been so successful. "When you connect people with these fantastic artworks or objects, you start to open up the purpose of the objects as well as the building. This immediately creates all these layers – living and breathing what the city and its culture is about. We want this to be a place of reflection and dialogue. Learning is important to us. We don't just want a passive audience, we want people to feel this is their museum and their collection. Traditional museums have a pitch that they have something important that they want people to know, but those people also have something to teach us, it's a two-way street. If we're fully engaged with our audiences, we should be learning from them all the time. Different generations of visitors are leaving their mark on the museum. They're leaving their opinion, their responses. That contributes to the growth of the museum. We're developing together."

The museum is more than just the objects. The galleries grow with the audiences, prompting better engagement and more meaningful exchange. There are programmes to collect memories through oral histories, to ensure those stories are collected for the future. The McManus' job is to reflect the city and the citizens and to allow them a mirror to see and examine their lives, past and present. That gives us an understanding of who our audience is, but then gives us a better understanding of who we are. That relationship, with the community and the city, is central to keeping The McManus relevant and at the heart of Dundee.

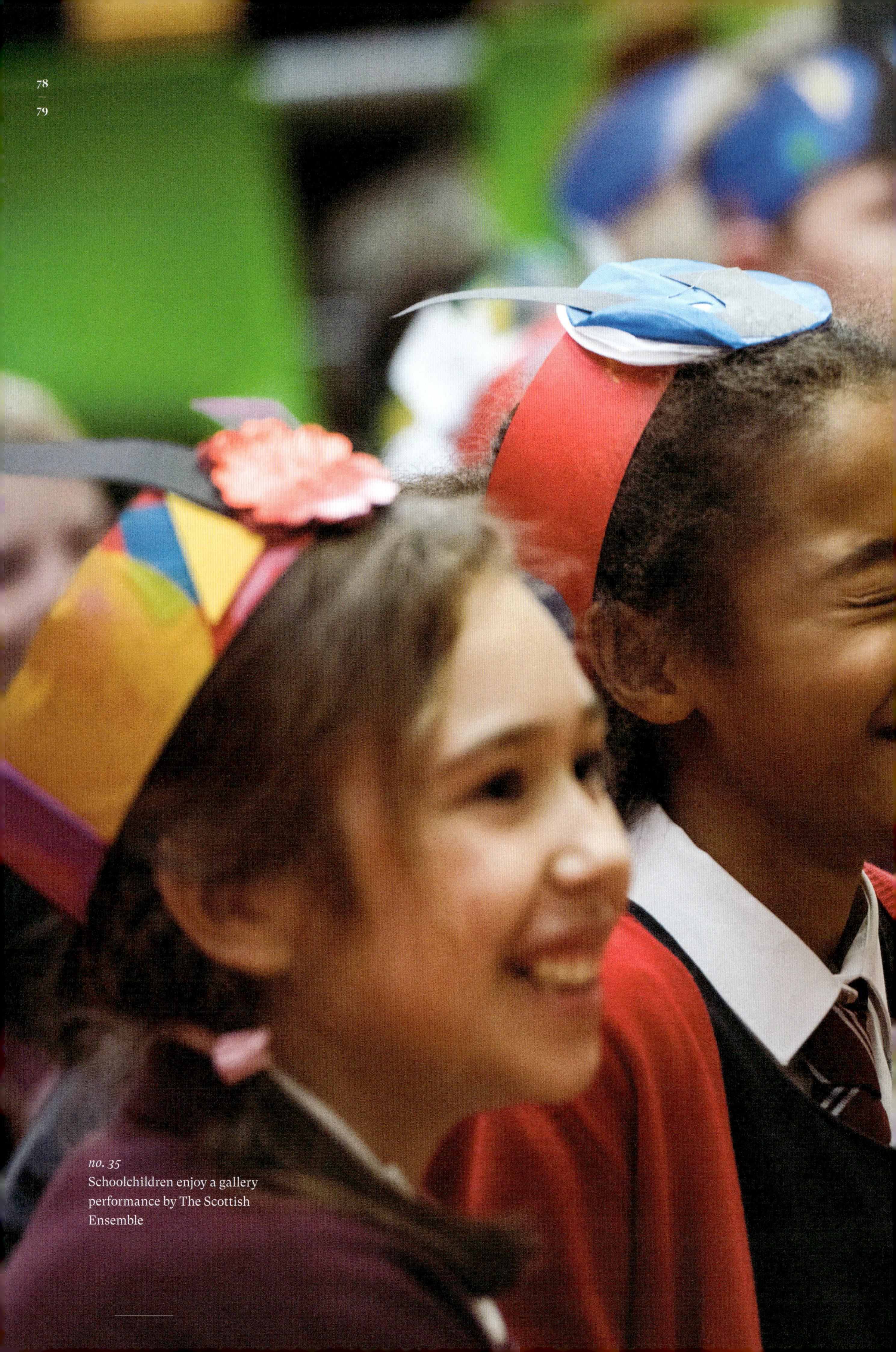

no. 35
Schoolchildren enjoy a gallery performance by The Scottish Ensemble

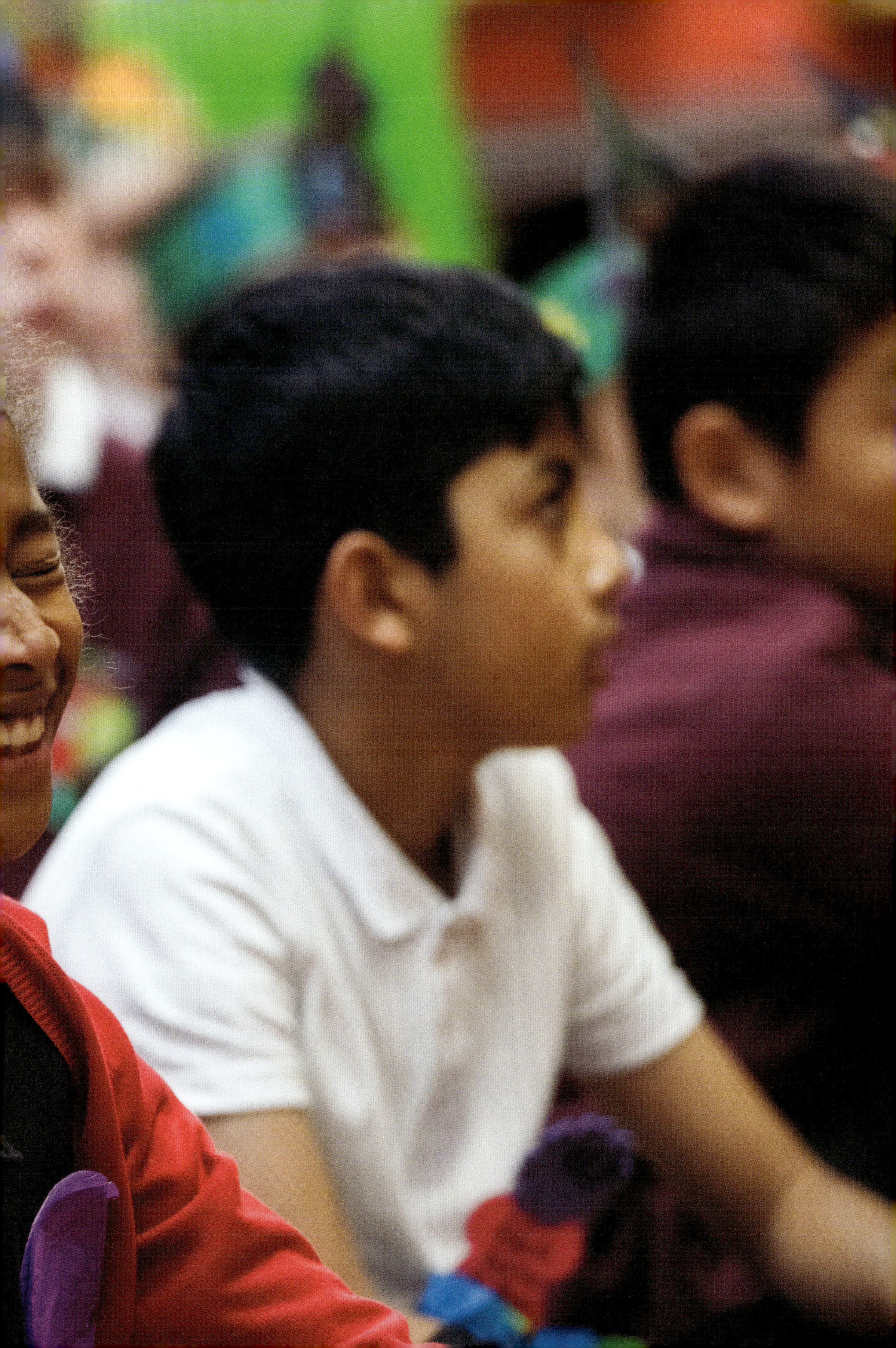

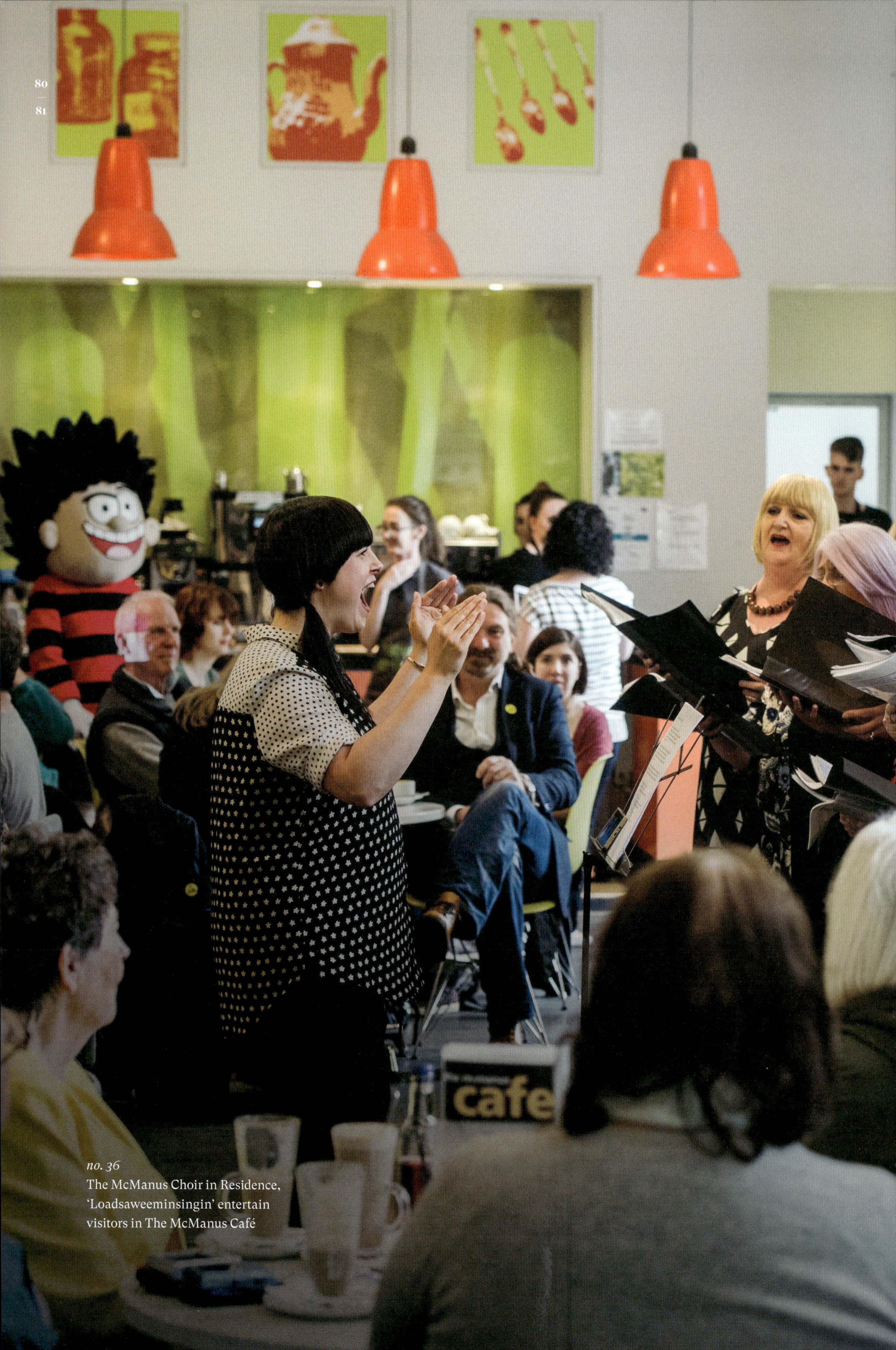

no. 36
The McManus Choir in Residence, 'Loadsaweeminsingin' entertain visitors in The McManus Café

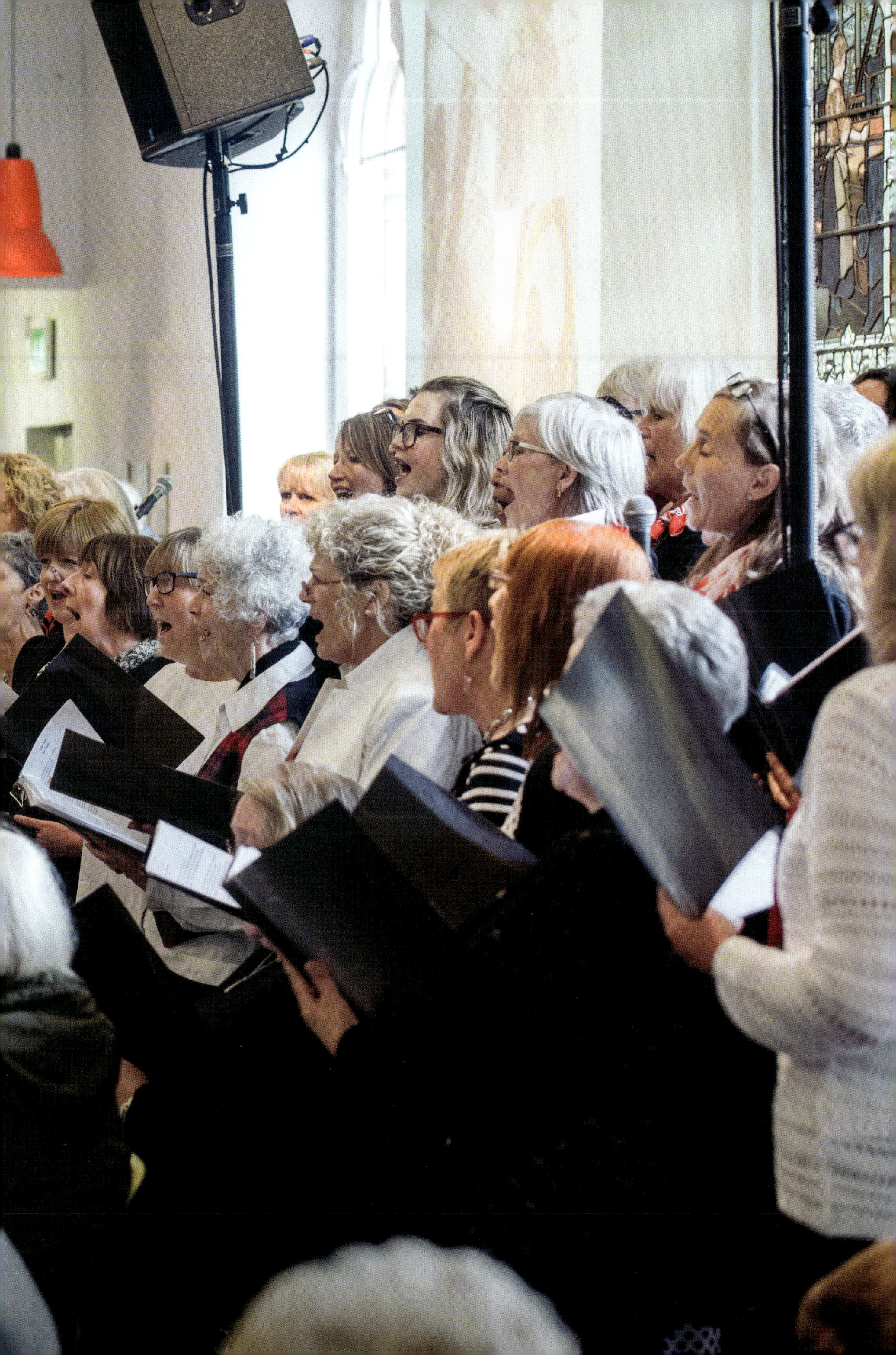

Gillian Easson

Executive Director,
Creative Dundee

Waldella, Dundee
by David Batchelor, 2009

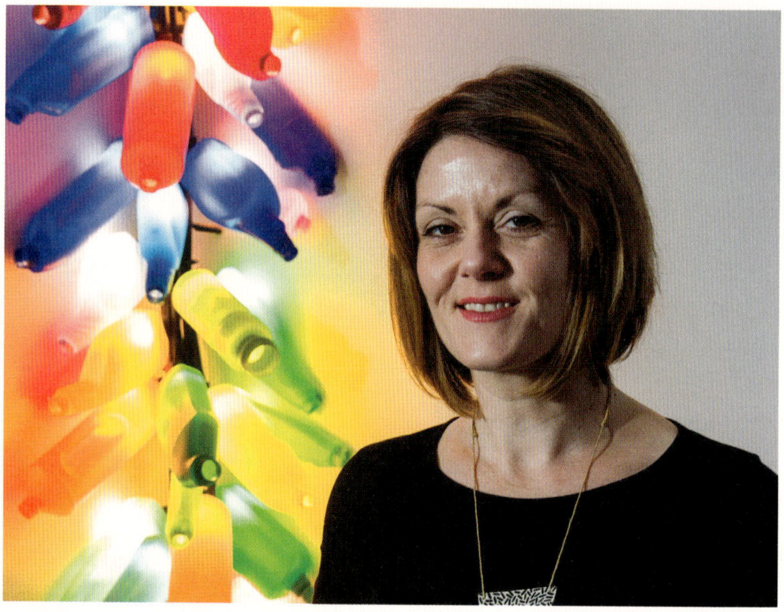

The McManus has always been a part of my family's life. My mum used to work there before I was born.

The McManus has always been a part of my family's life. My Mum used to work there before I was born in the Reference Library, in the old Albert Institute. I remember visiting as I grew up vividly – running up the stairs, playing outside and exploring the spaces. But I was totally petrified of Queen Victoria; I fell off the bus seat one day as I was so scared of her – I had a childhood fear of statues.

It's Dundee's number one gem, the people's museum. It has been part of the fabric through the generations, managing to maintain its relevance. It's the first place that I take people who are new to the city – I bring them to the museum and take them to the 'Making of Modern Dundee' gallery, because it shows our industrial past succinctly and it has an eye on where the future is heading too. The Creative Learning team reach out across the city, keeping people engaged with the space no matter where you live.

I picked David Batchelor's Waldella as the object I enjoy the most. I wanted to select something that has a connection to Dundee but has a unique style too. David Batchelor was born in 1955 in Dundee, and I think there are 300 or 400 bottles within the piece. I love that when you turn the corner, the piece is there, illuminating the space like a beacon, exuding happiness. The building encapsulates the contemporary and the traditional and this piece somehow joins them together. I love the preservation that goes into it too – the plastic bottles disintegrate quite quickly, so the team are always looking out online for exact replicas of the bottles to replace those that are decomposing. It's a big conservation job and I think that's fascinating the care and consideration given to all objects in the brilliant collection.

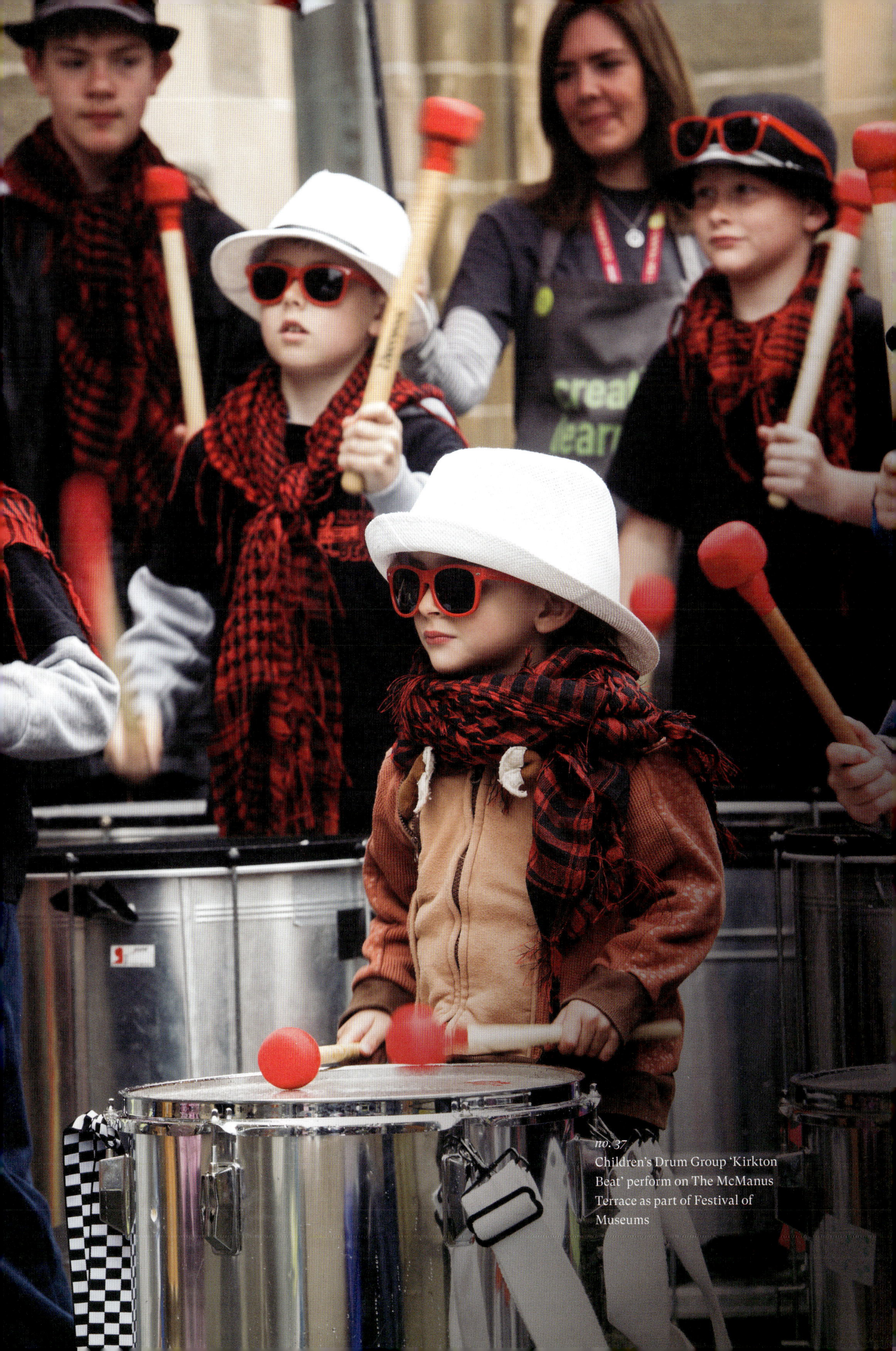

no. 37
Children's Drum Group 'Kirkton Beat' perform on The McManus Terrace as part of Festival of Museums

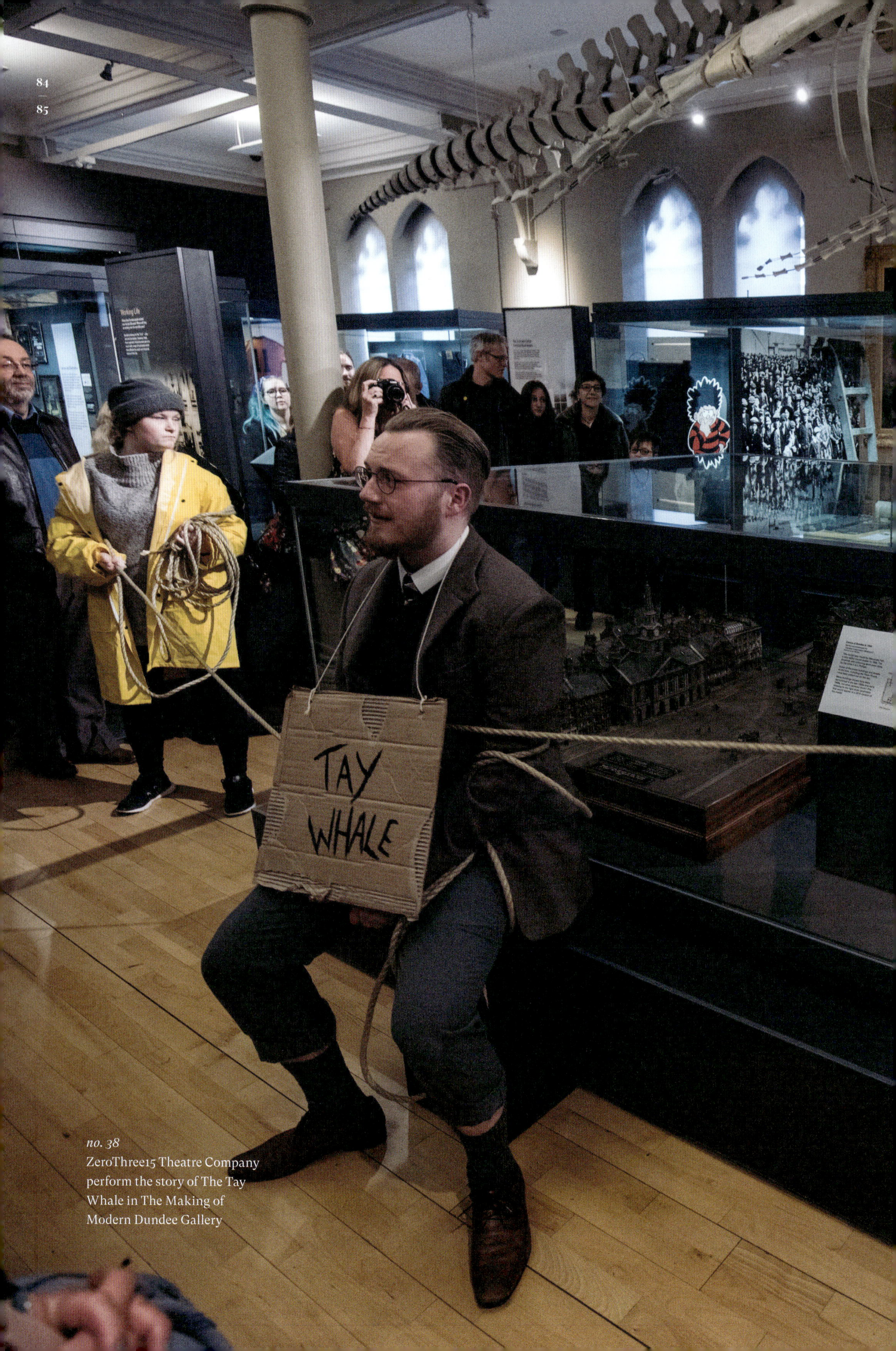

no. 38
ZeroThree15 Theatre Company perform the story of The Tay Whale in The Making of Modern Dundee Gallery

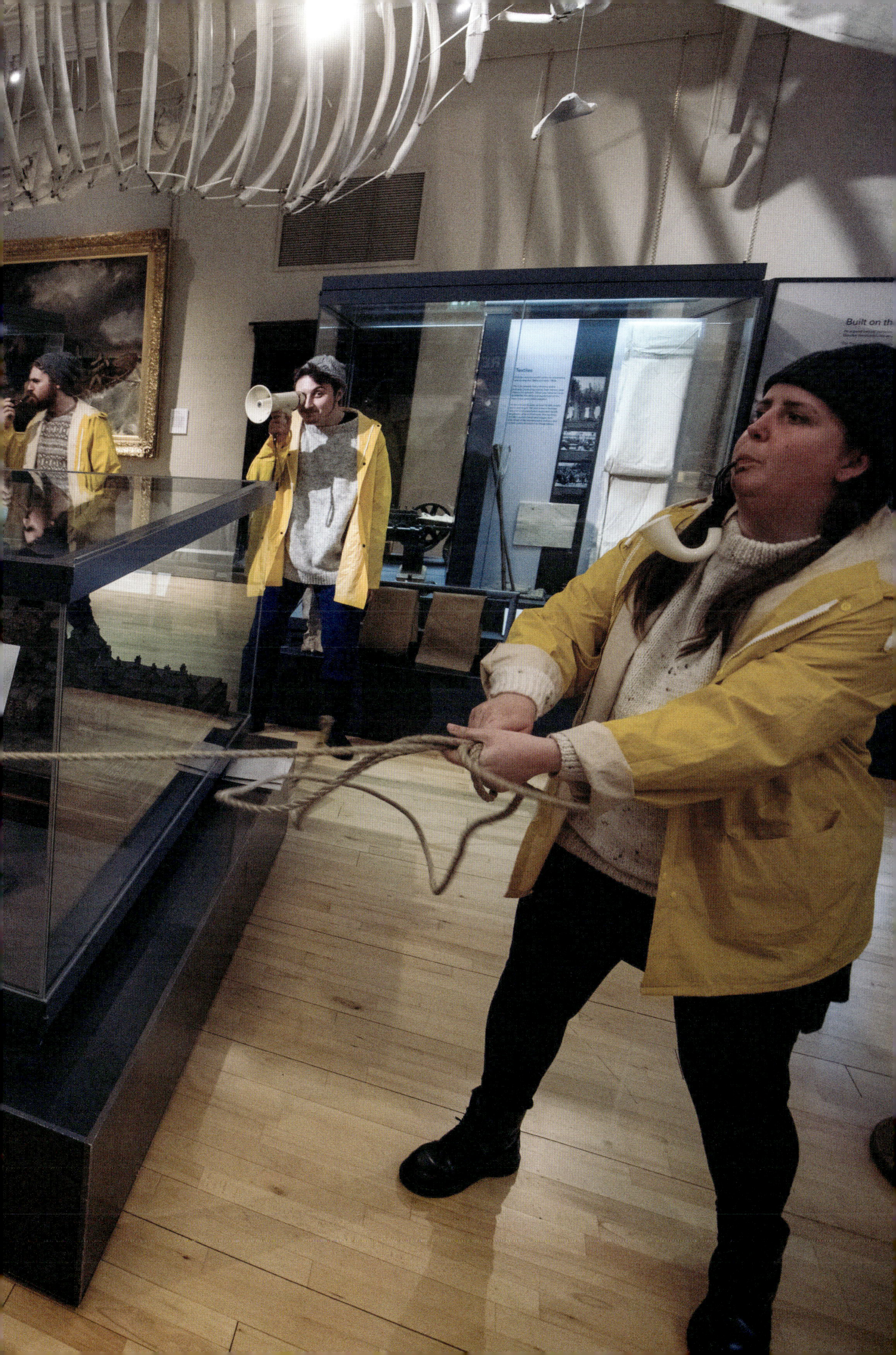

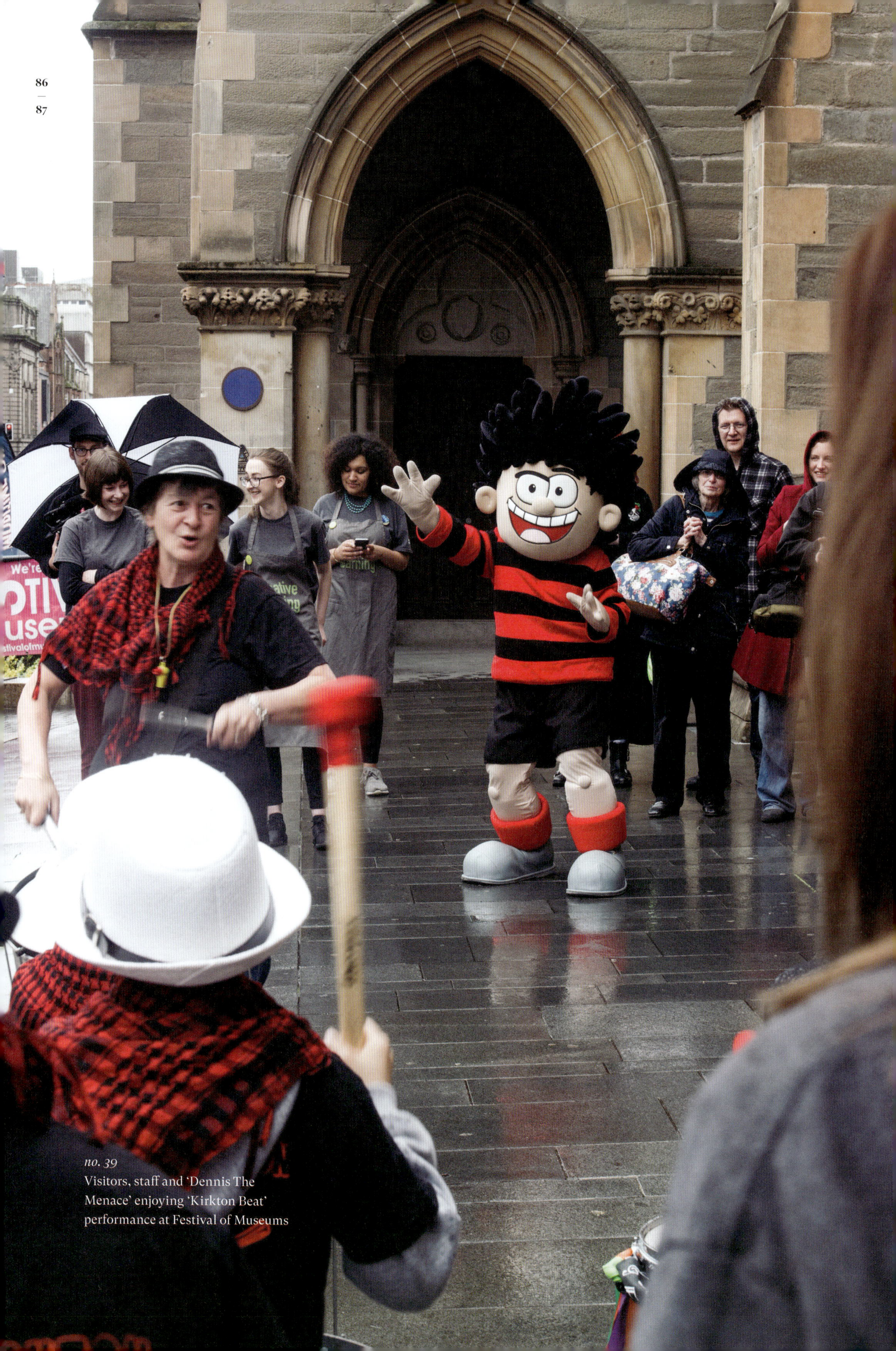

no. 39
Visitors, staff and 'Dennis The Menace' enjoying 'Kirkton Beat' performance at Festival of Museums

Stewart Murdoch

Managing Director
Leisure and Culture Dundee

Brass Mariner's Astrolabe, 1555

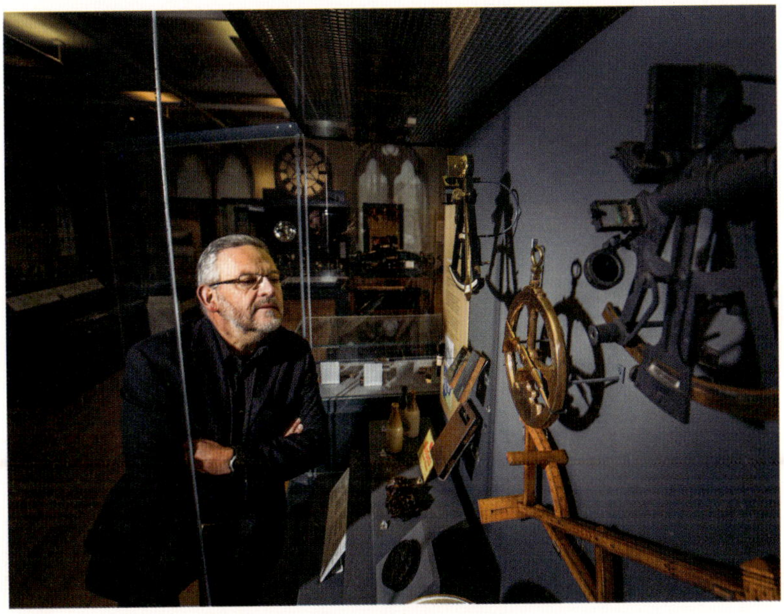

A building which has its own fascinating story... tells the story of this city beautifully.

I had both the privilege and the challenge of being the Director of Leisure, Arts and Heritage when The McManus was totally redeveloped. This was a huge and complex project. The building was in perilous condition structurally.

As is often the nature of a project of this nature, it was only once the building was emptied and properly examined the full extent of the challenge was evident. It also became clear that doing any piling would potentially initiate further damage and a unique design solution would have to be devised. The engineers devised a solution which involved creating a concrete raft both inside and round the perimeter of the building.

The result is one of the best mid-scale galleries and museums in the UK. A building which has its own fascinating story, housing a collection which tells the story of this city beautifully. Like the foundations which support the building much of this work is unseen, but like the foundations it is essential and without it we would not have the thoughtful displays and interpretation that our visitors take for granted. The privilege has been an insight into the engineering and the curation, which for most is unseen.

The astrolobe is the object that perfectly summarises Dundee's place in the world. It was found – it wasn't made in Dundee. It comes from the captain of a Portuguese ship and it's a very early navigational instrument. It demonstrates Dundee's European and international connections.

I like its materiality, it's made in brass. It was a forgotten part of the collection. It was only when a curator did some digging on the history of the object that its story and value was properly realised.

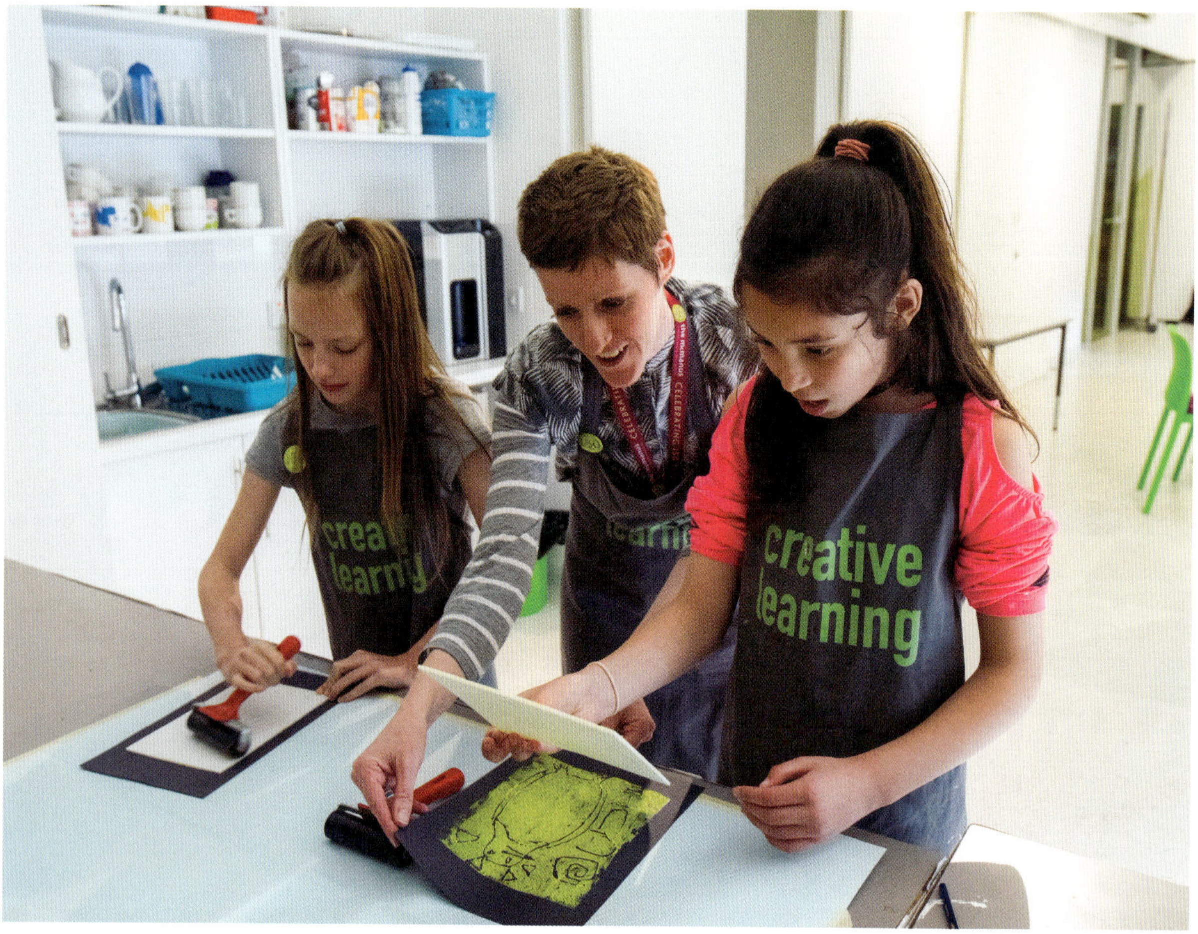

no. 40
Printmaking in The Creative
Learning Studio

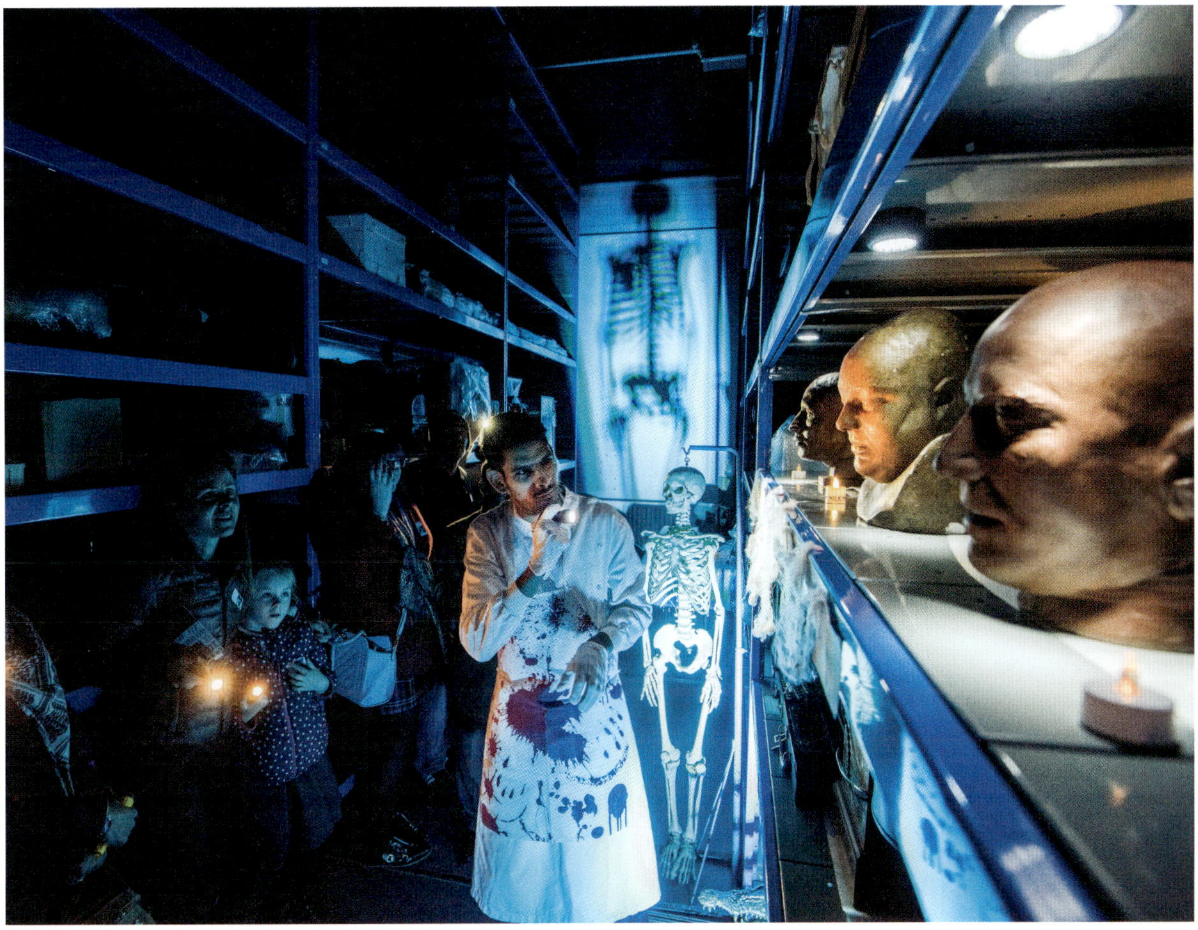

no. 41
Hallowe'en Behind the Scenes Tour at the Collections Unit showcasing some of the more unusual and scary objects

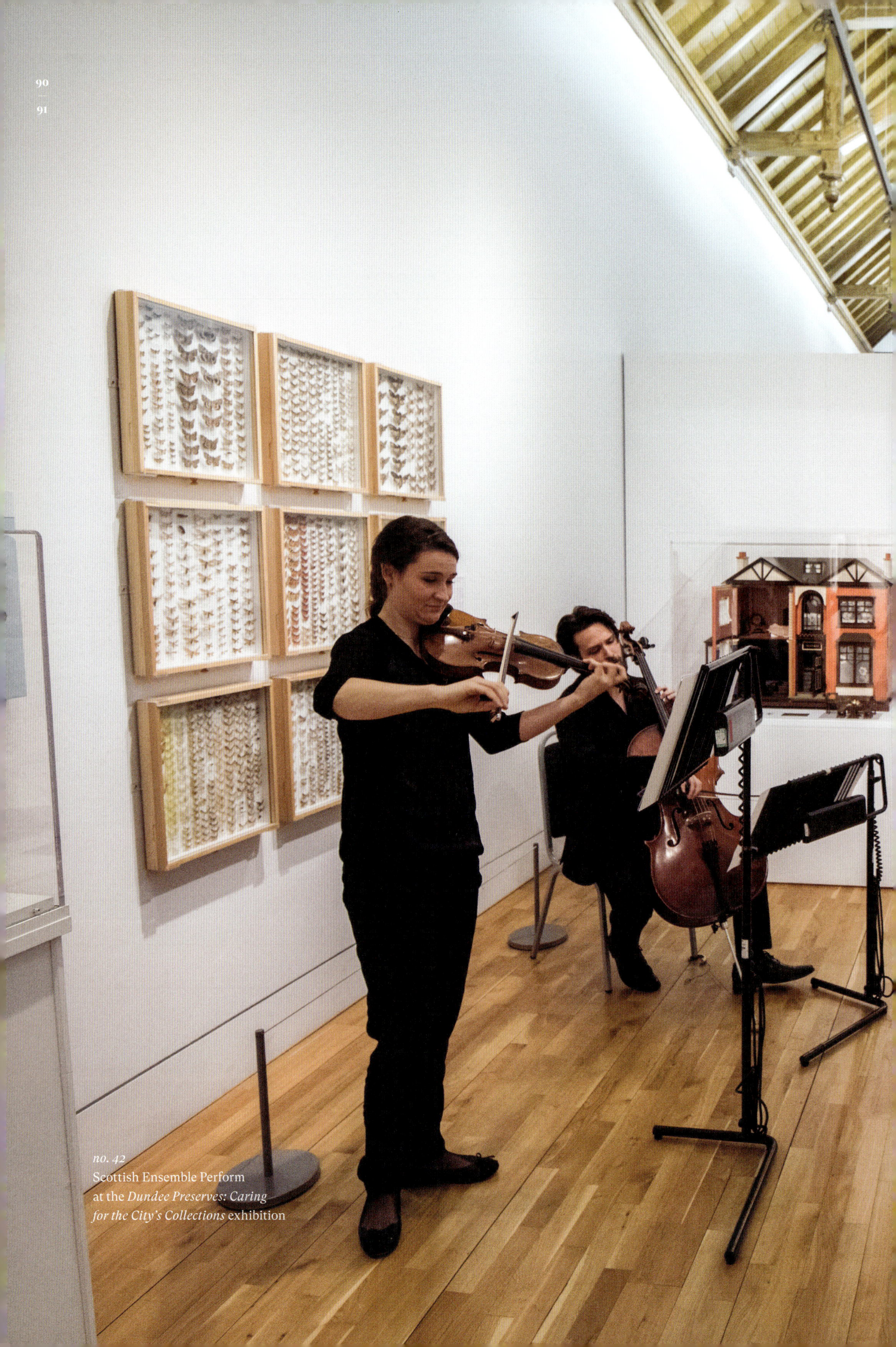

no. 42
Scottish Ensemble Perform at the *Dundee Preserves: Caring for the City's Collections* exhibition

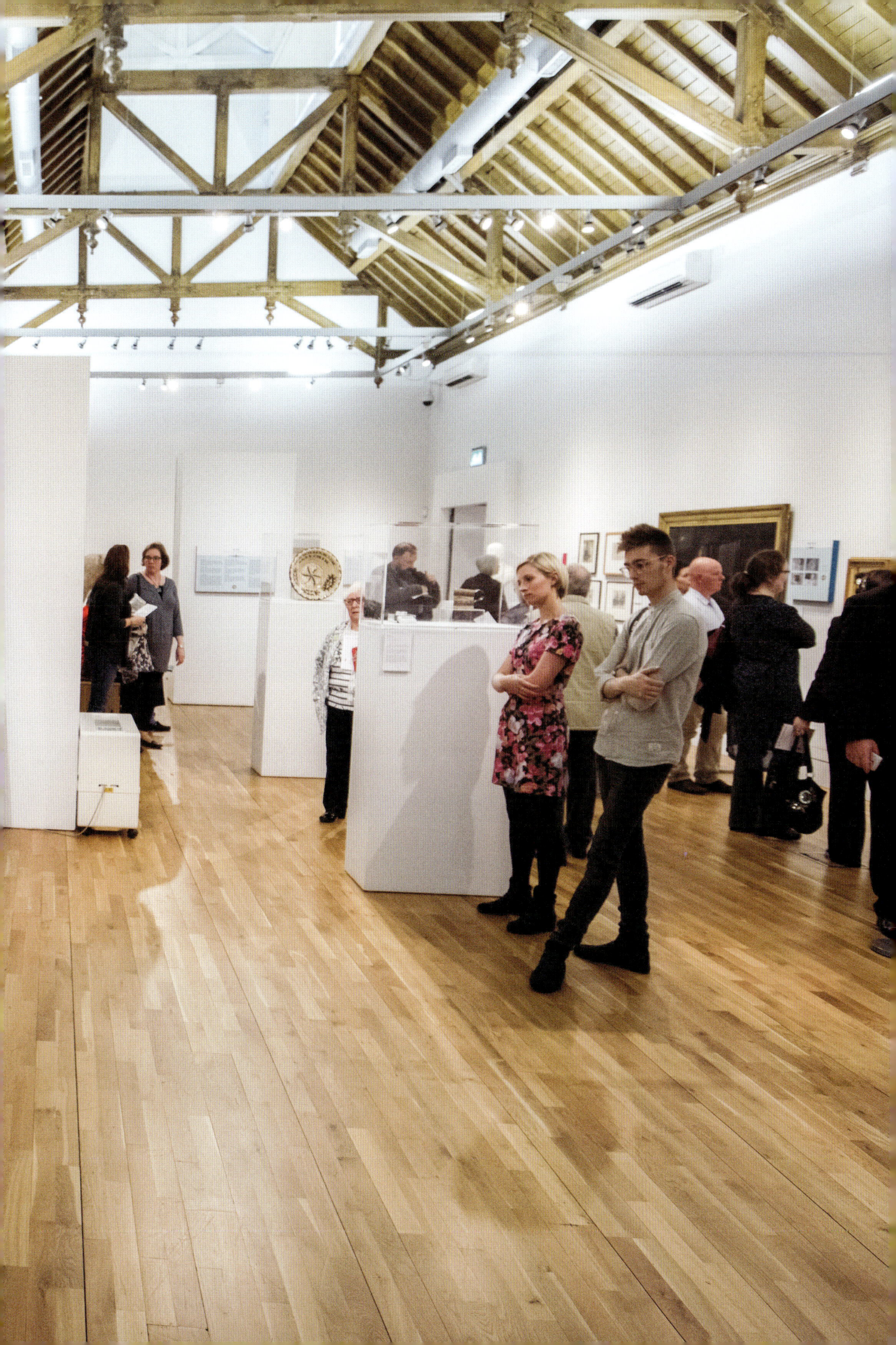

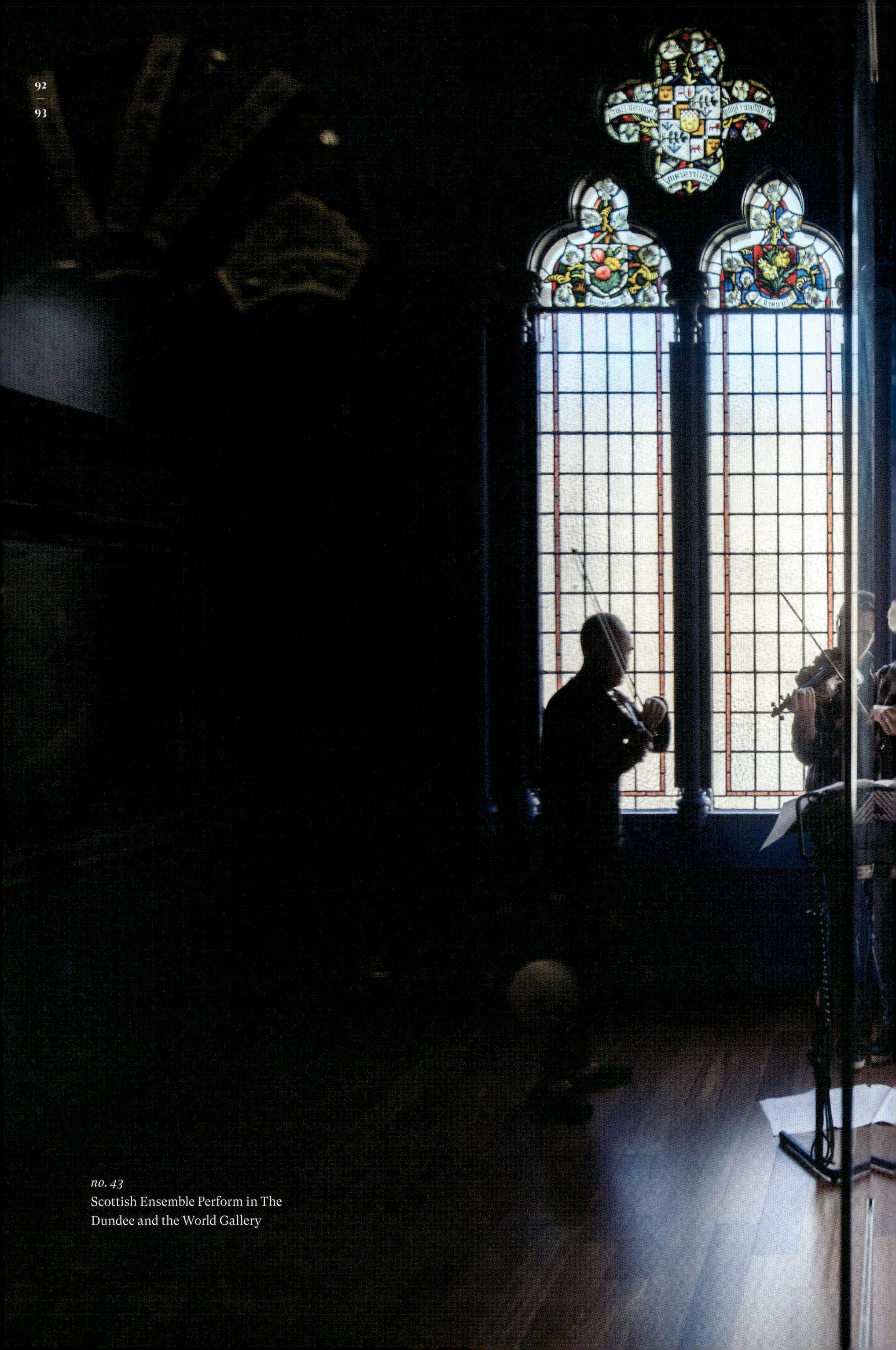

no. 43
Scottish Ensemble Perform in The Dundee and the World Gallery

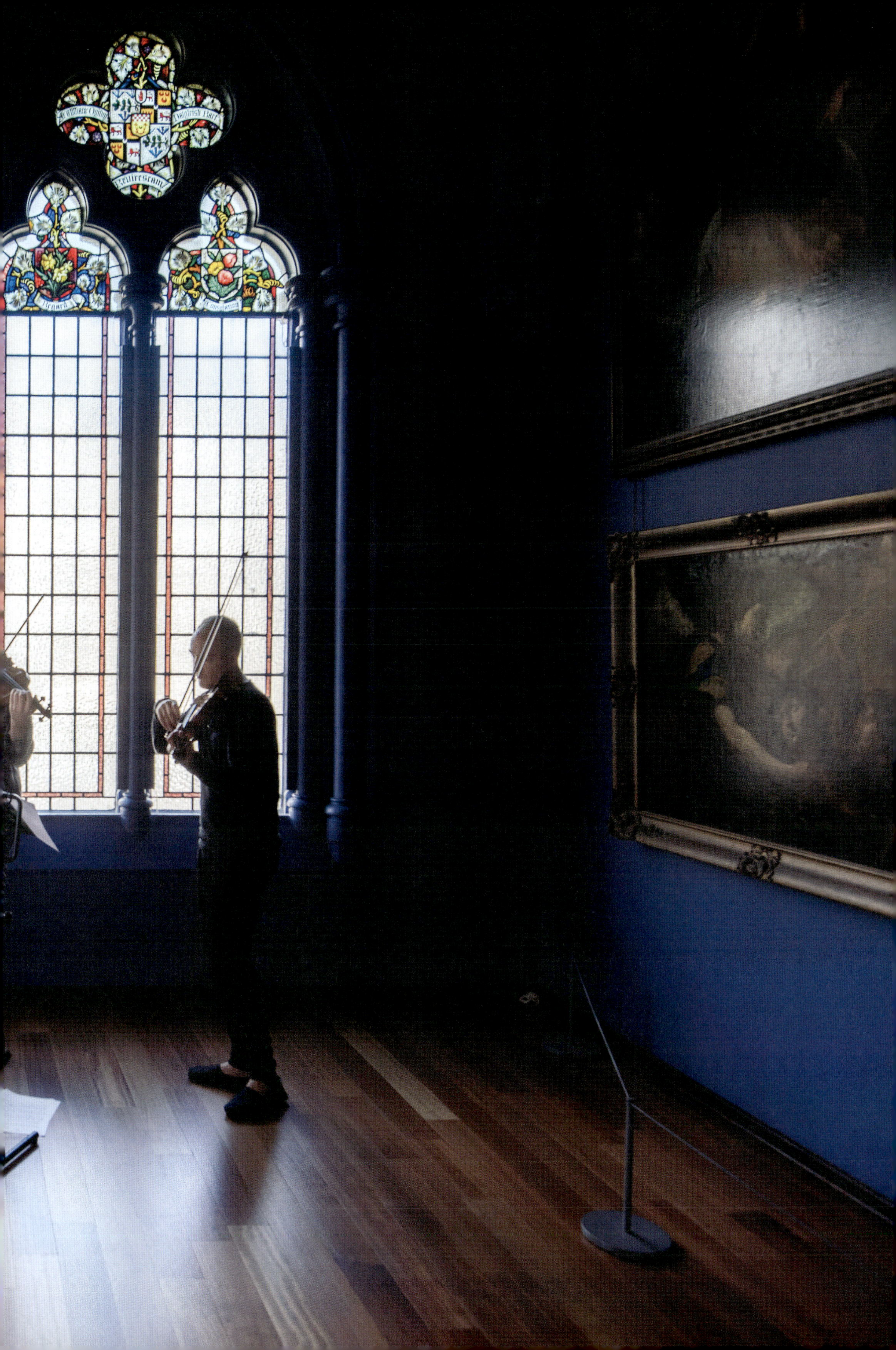

Bob Duncan

Former Lord Provost

The McManus

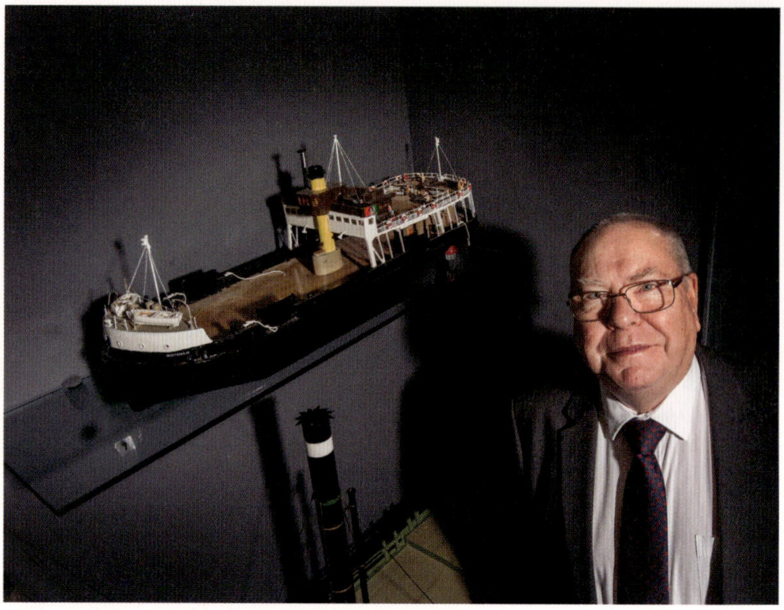

It's a place where people gather, talk and learn.

The McManus is the heart of Dundee. It's a place where people gather, talk and learn. Generations of Dundonians have been coming here, time after time, to bring their children and grandchildren. I love the building itself – it's grand and imposing but still manages to be welcoming. The exhibitions are always excellent and the staff give the warmest of welcomes.

Whatever changes happen in the city, as things shift and Dundee develops, McManus will always have a place in the heart of the place and the people.

I was lucky enough to be involved in the reopening of The McManus as a councillor and as the Chair of Leisure and Culture Dundee. It was a unique opportunity to create a world class museum and the team made the absolute most of that chance. I remember the day it reopened and how proud the people of Dundee were. It had taken time and money, but it was worth it. Thousands flocked to The McManus after it reopened and it hosted paintings by Titian and drawings by Leonardo Da Vinci.

It's the items that are from Dundee that are the most special, however. They're the pieces that tell our story. The story of Dundee.

Whatever changes happen in the city, as things shift and Dundee continues to develop, The McManus will always have a place in the heart of the place and the people. I hope all the new visitors to the city make time to come and see this gem while they're here.

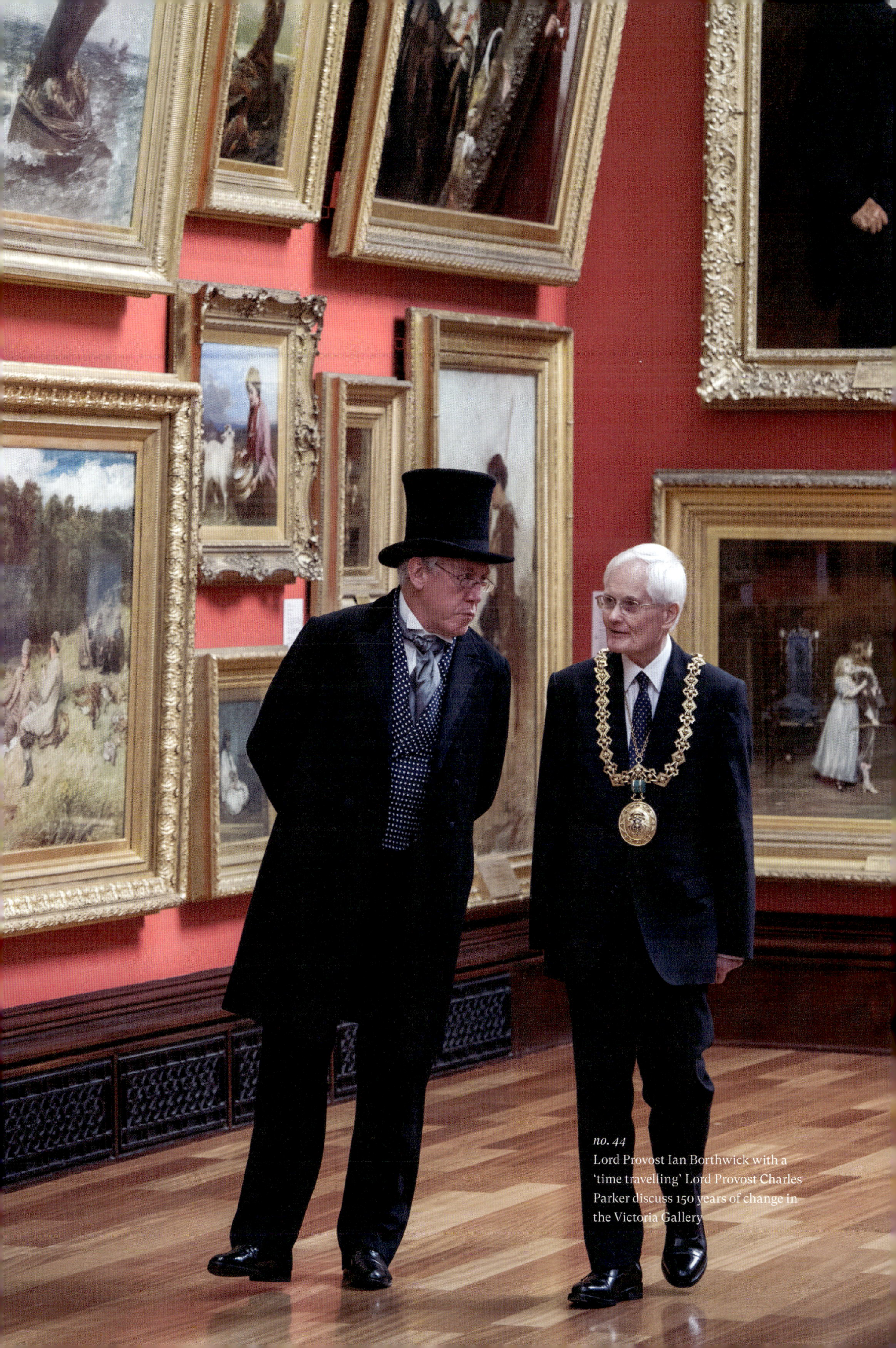

no. 44
Lord Provost Ian Borthwick with a 'time travelling' Lord Provost Charles Parker discuss 150 years of change in the Victoria Gallery

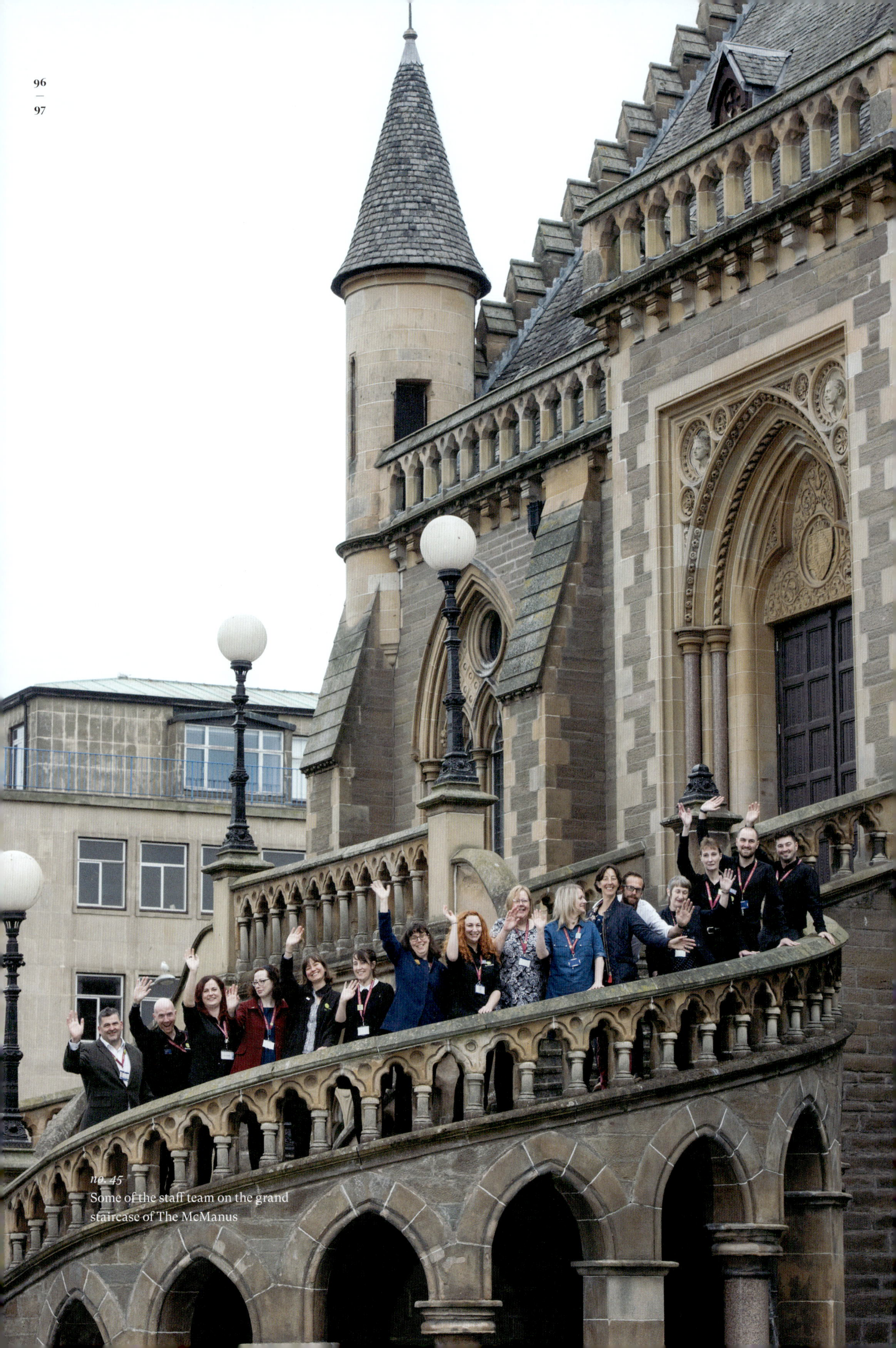

no. 45
Some of the staff team on the grand staircase of The McManus

Kerry McAlpine

Volunteer, McManus Learning and Engagement

Creative Learning Studio

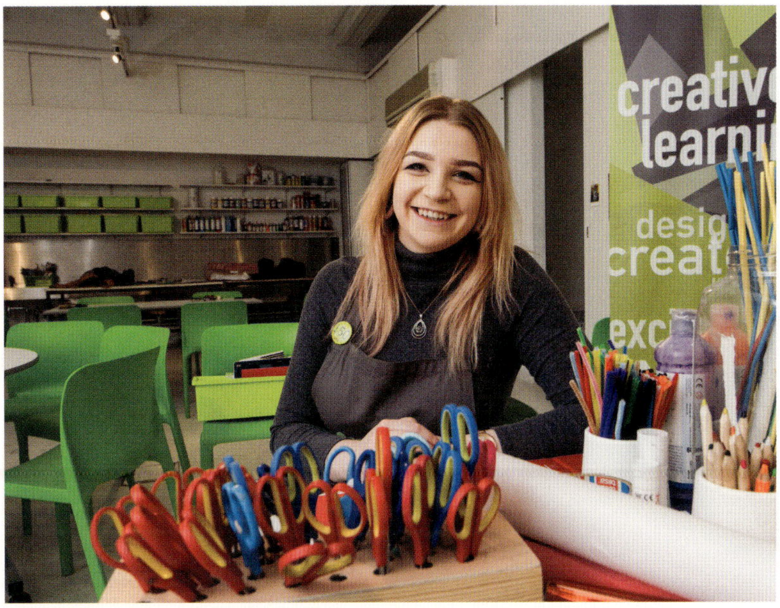

The Learning and Engagement team here are brilliant, they've been so supportive.

I started coming to The McManus as part of the Youth Action Group. I was looking for a way to get to know the city and when I saw the building and the contents, I was completely blown away. When I finished my college course, I asked if I could volunteer on a more regular basis.

The Learning and Engagement team here are brilliant, they've been so supportive and helped with giving me time to work on my portfolio. Volunteering here has also helped increase my confidence so much, helped with interviews and making me believe in myself – now I've got a place at Duncan of Jordanstone College of Art and Design, part of the University of Dundee."

I chose the Learning Studio as my favourite part of the museum. I work in here with the team or alone. It's a lovely welcoming space, whether it's full of kids or just us, having a meeting. When it's full, I get a rush of energy, it's so busy. I didn't expect this experience to open so many doors. I've met people from all over the city, different artists, different communities. Some people see volunteering as unpaid work, but there's no comparison.

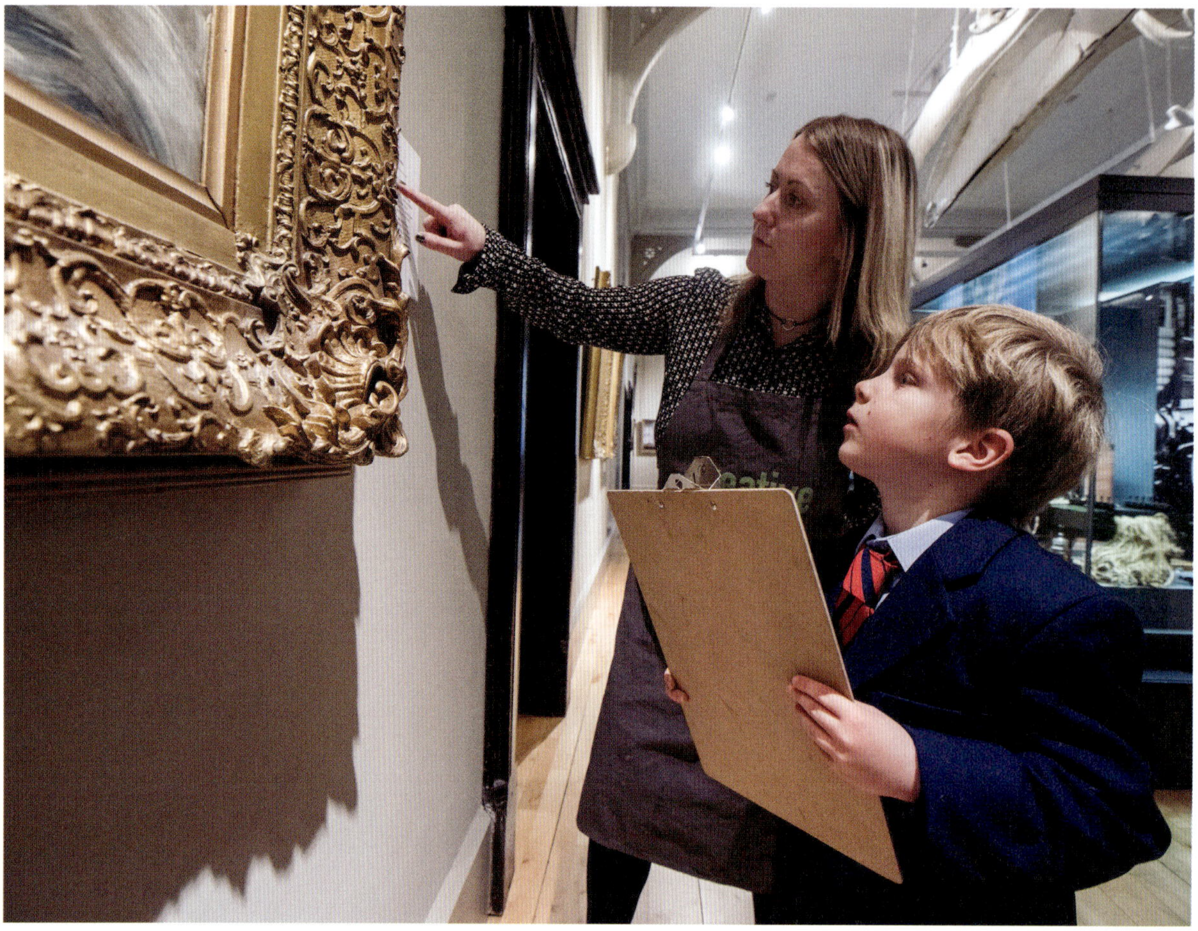

no. 46
A young visitor researching the collection with The Creative Learning Team

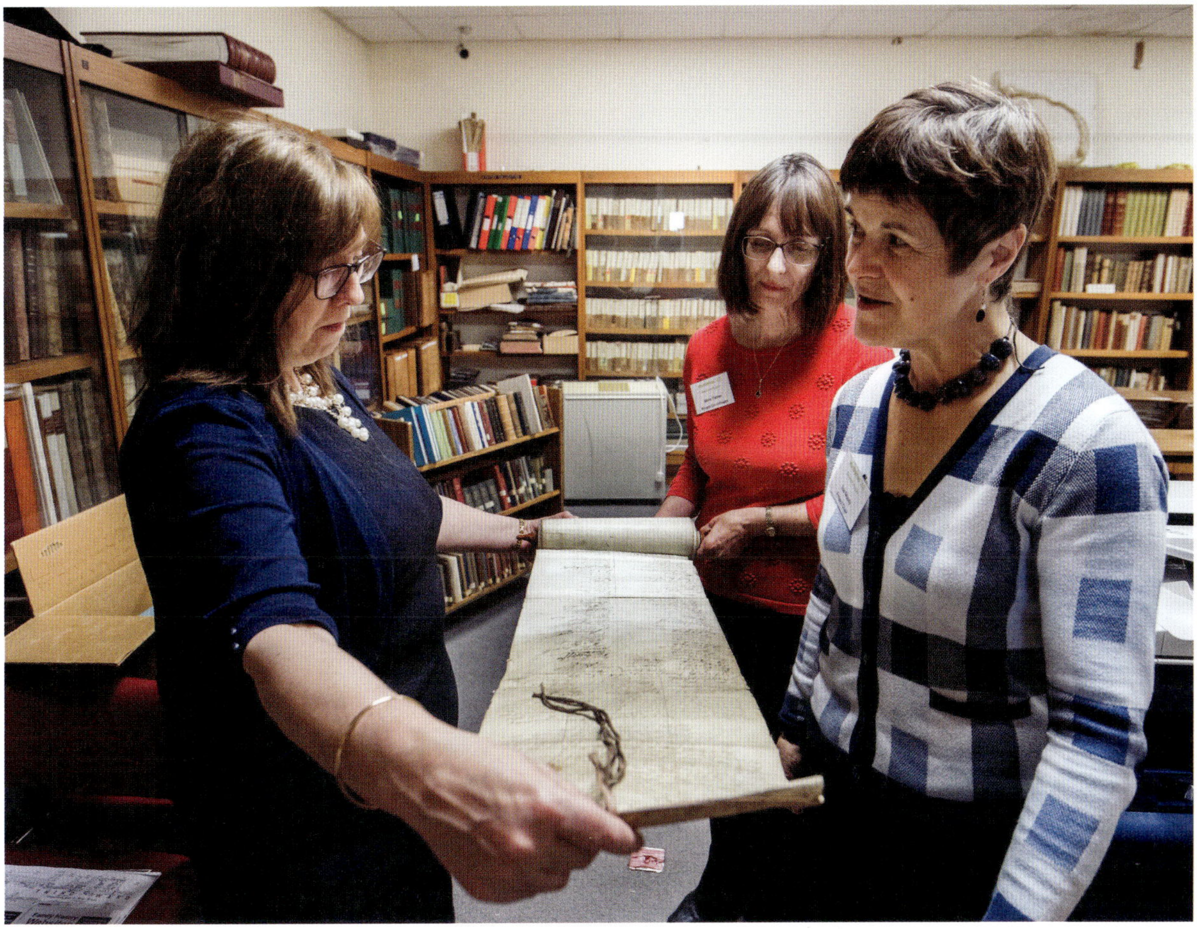

no. 47
The McManus 168 group viewing the list of original subscribers to the creation of the Albert Institute in 1867

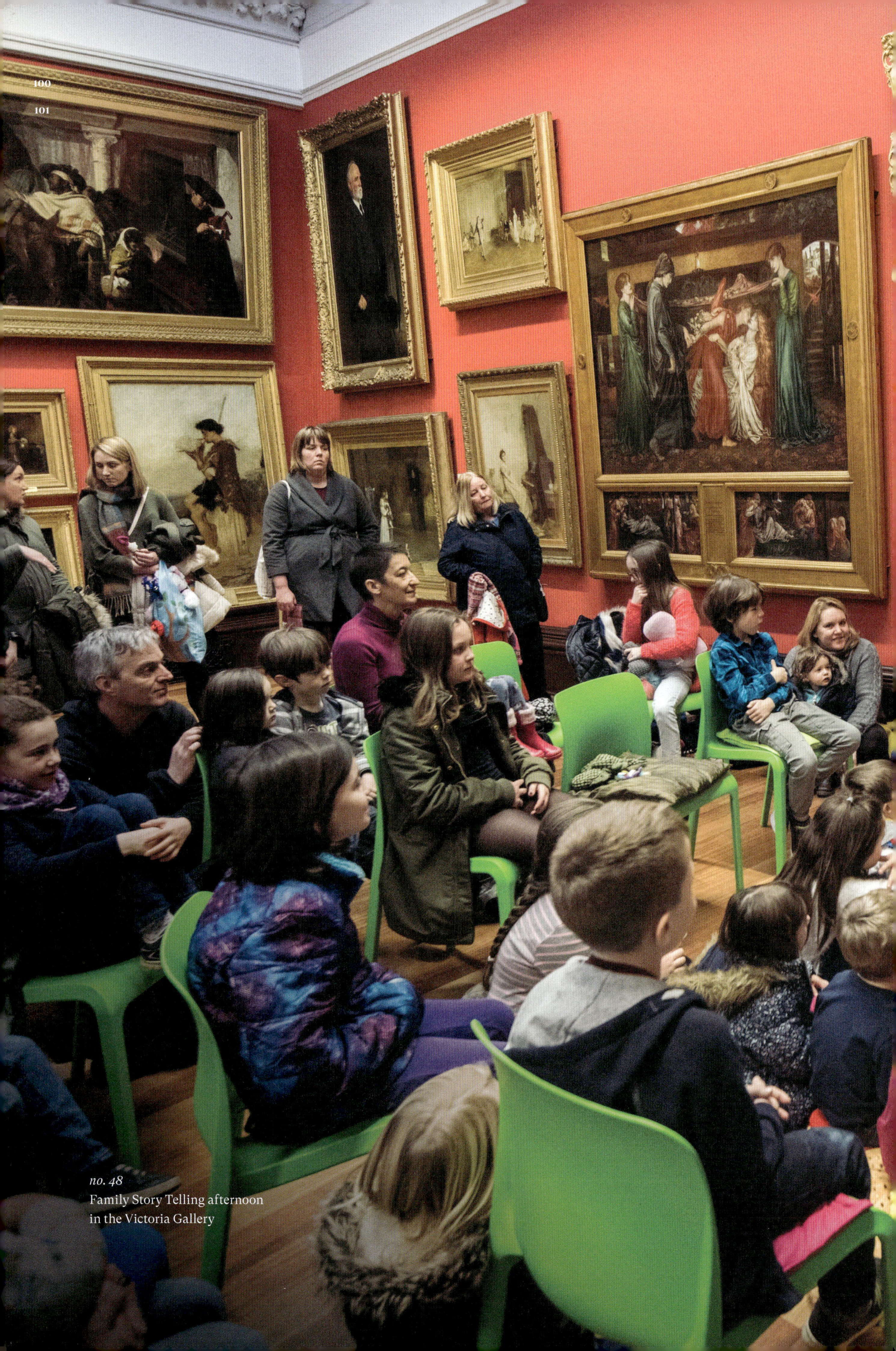

no. 48
Family Story Telling afternoon
in the Victoria Gallery

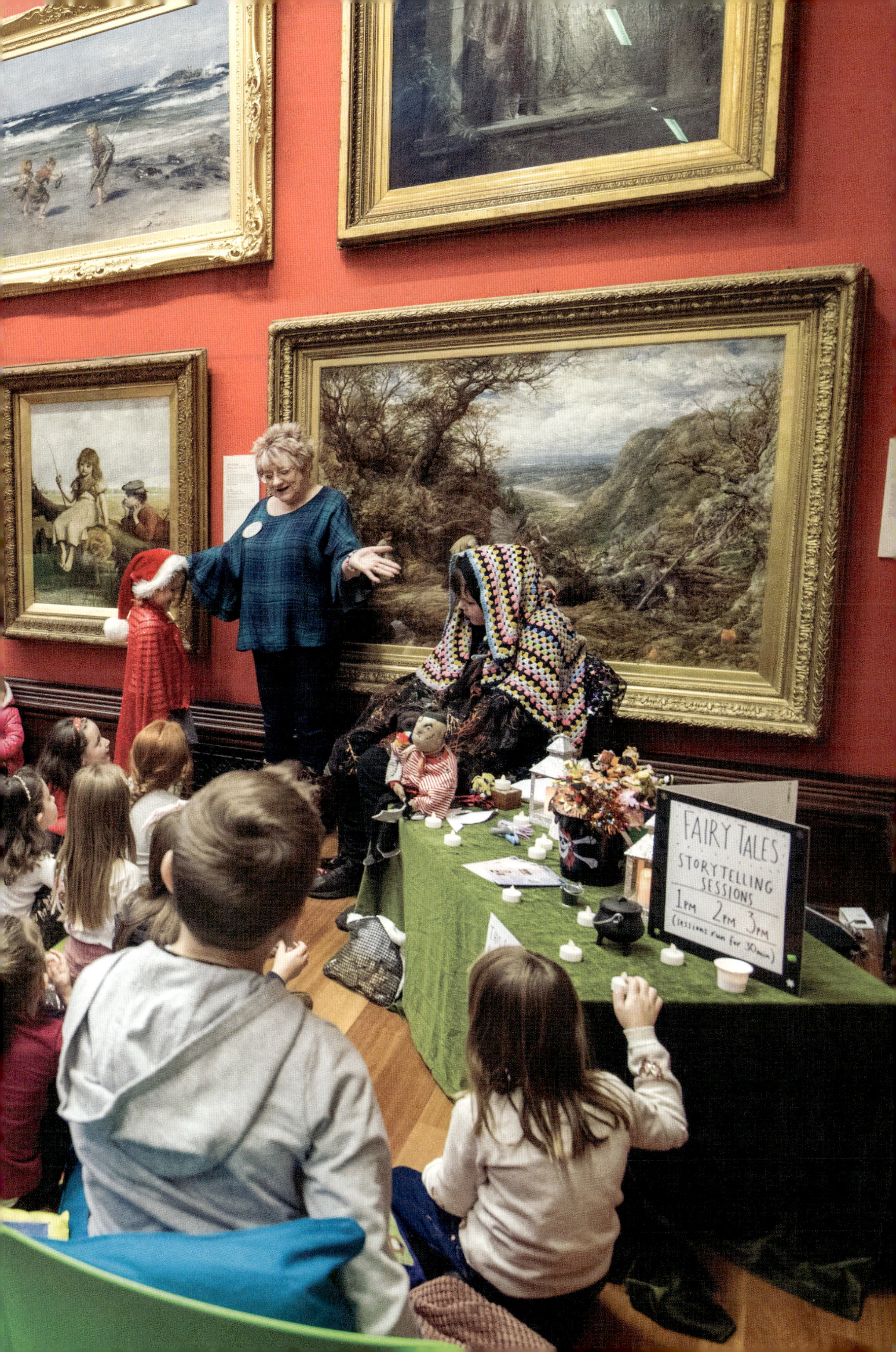
FAIRY TALES
STORYTELLING SESSIONS
1PM 2PM 3PM
(sessions run for 30mins)

Sue Moody

Chair of The McManus
168 Group

Duchess of Argyll, nee Elizabeth Gunning, Duchess of Hamilton, 1770, Catherine Read

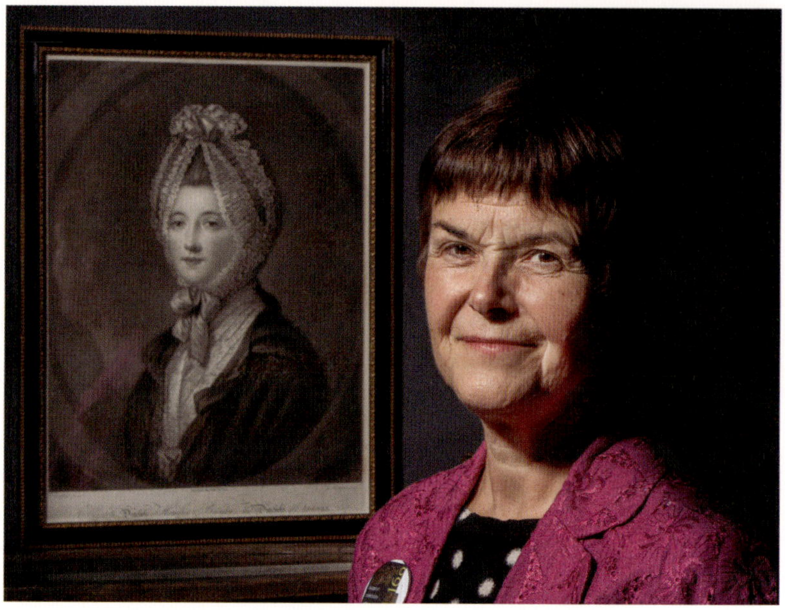

Both these women are remarkable and fit well with the notion of Dundee where women flourish.

I'm the chair of The McManus 168 group, the supporters' group for the museum. The biggest thing we've been doing is a project about the original subscribers. We're called the 168 group because we originally thought that's how many people subscribed to create the Albert Institute. But our research has uncovered 261 so far! We've no plans to change our name.

The project to uncover the stories of all the people who made the Albert Institute a reality is an exciting one. We've involved historians, archivists, family history people, genealogists and we've recruited more than 100 volunteers who don't have any experience in this kind of research.

The object I've chosen is a mezzotint from 1770 by a female portrait painter called Catherine Read. Catherine was from Dundee and she made a good living as a painter, a very unusual occupation for women then. She moved to Paris, London and then India, where she died. I love to think of her travelling and painting. The portrait is of Elizabeth Gunning, Duchess of Hamilton and Argyll. Elizabeth was born in Ireland, to impoverished gentry – her father frittered away their money. Although they had a castle in Roscommon they were poor and she and her sister had to make their own living. In those days there were not many ways in which women could make money, so Elizabeth went on the stage in Dublin and became an actress. She attracted the attention of the Duke of Hamilton – she was a 16-year old beauty – and he proposed to her on the night they met. She became a Baroness in her own right, which was also unusual for her time, so I think she too was a force to be reckoned with.

Both these women are remarkable and fit well with the notion of Dundee where women flourish and are important in their own right. The conversations between them would certainly have been interesting!

Tom Normand

Art Historian

Young Girl with Red Hair, Alan Fletcher

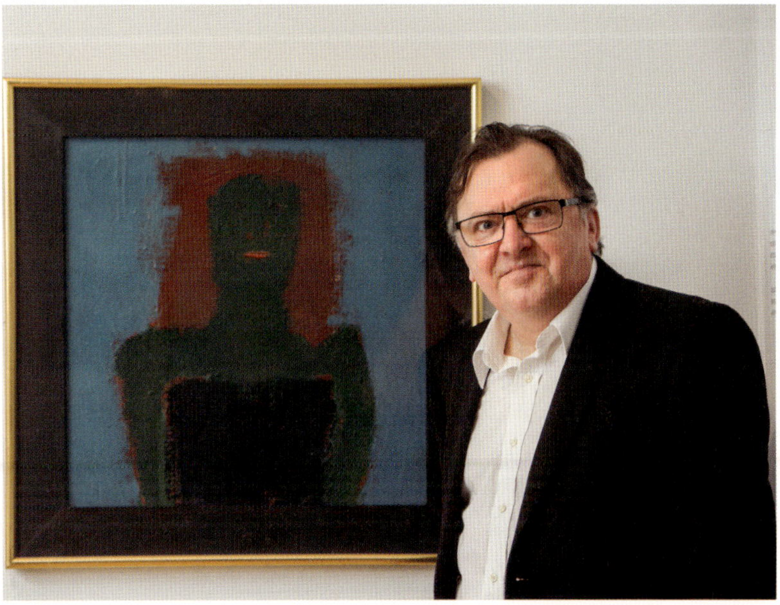

I've always thought of The McManus Galleries as a giant treasure-house.

I've always thought of The McManus as a giant treasure-house. Full of every kind of artwork and object: from the finest of fine art, to the most intriguing of curiosities, and on to the familiar – perhaps half-forgotten – handiworks from everyday life and culture.

As a gallery, and a museum, it achieves that special mission. It represents local life and the work, experience and accomplishments of Dundee people. But, it also connects with the global world and with the deep history of Tayside. And so it reaches back into Palaeolithic times and journeys – by way of geology, ethnography, zoology, and scientific achievements – to the world of modern Scotland, with all its variety.

For my part I've been most engaged with the collections of art, and especially paintings. Teaching art history at the University of St Andrews I'd often bring students to The McManus to view the fine collection of 19th century paintings, bequeathed to the gallery by James Guthrie Orchar. And, to experience the rich trove of 20th century painting. For more than twenty years I'd also bring groups of American students, attending the St Andrews University Summer School, to the galleries and there they'd be introduced to a complete history of Scottish life, culture and art. They were never disappointed.

My selected object is Alan Fletcher's Young Girl with Red Hair, an oil on board, from circa 1957. Fletcher has been largely neglected within the Scottish canon perhaps because he died tragically young, in 1958, at the age of 28. But The McManus is lucky enough to hold three of his works; this portrait, and two stunning still-life paintings. It is a privilege shared with few other galleries in Scotland.

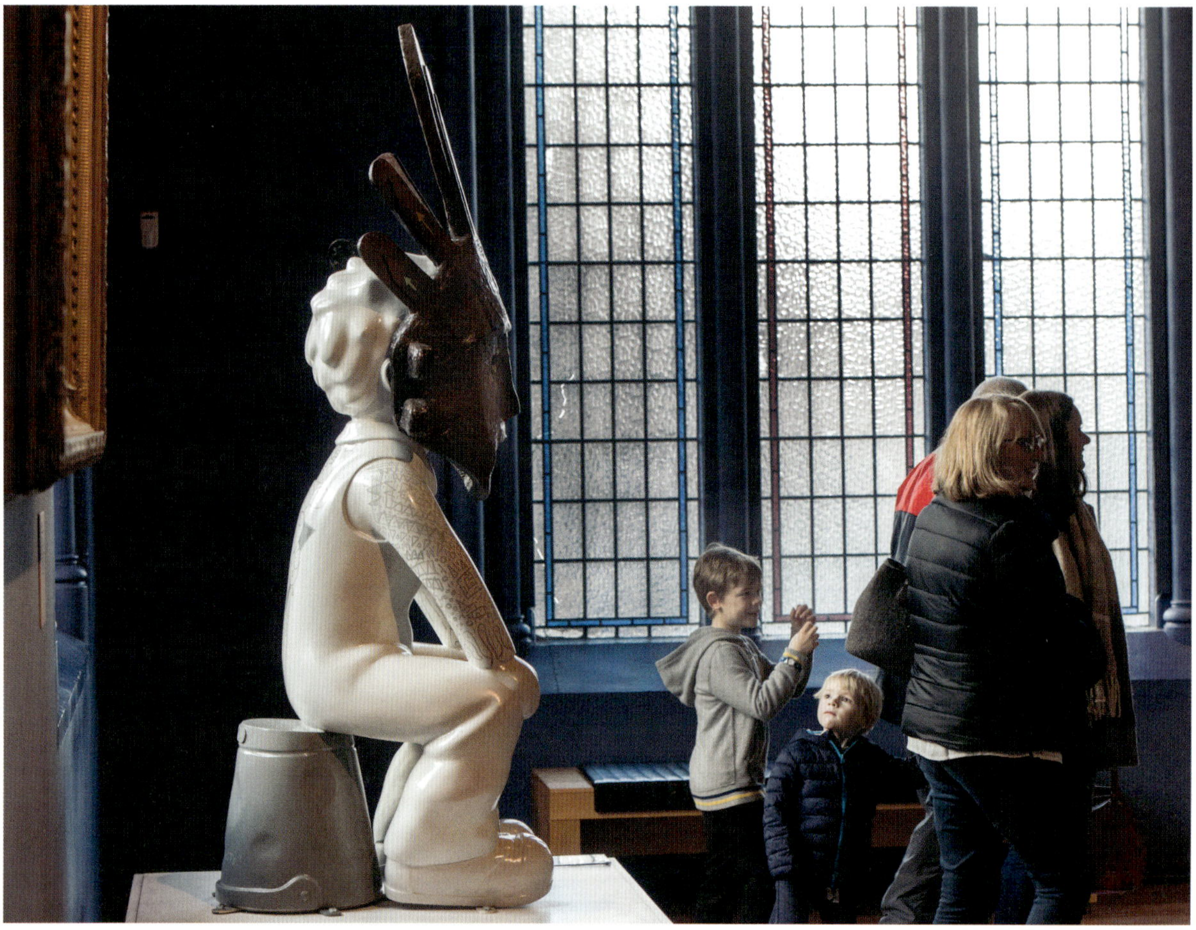

no. 49
Oor Wullie with his McManus
inspired mask becoming
Oor Artefacts

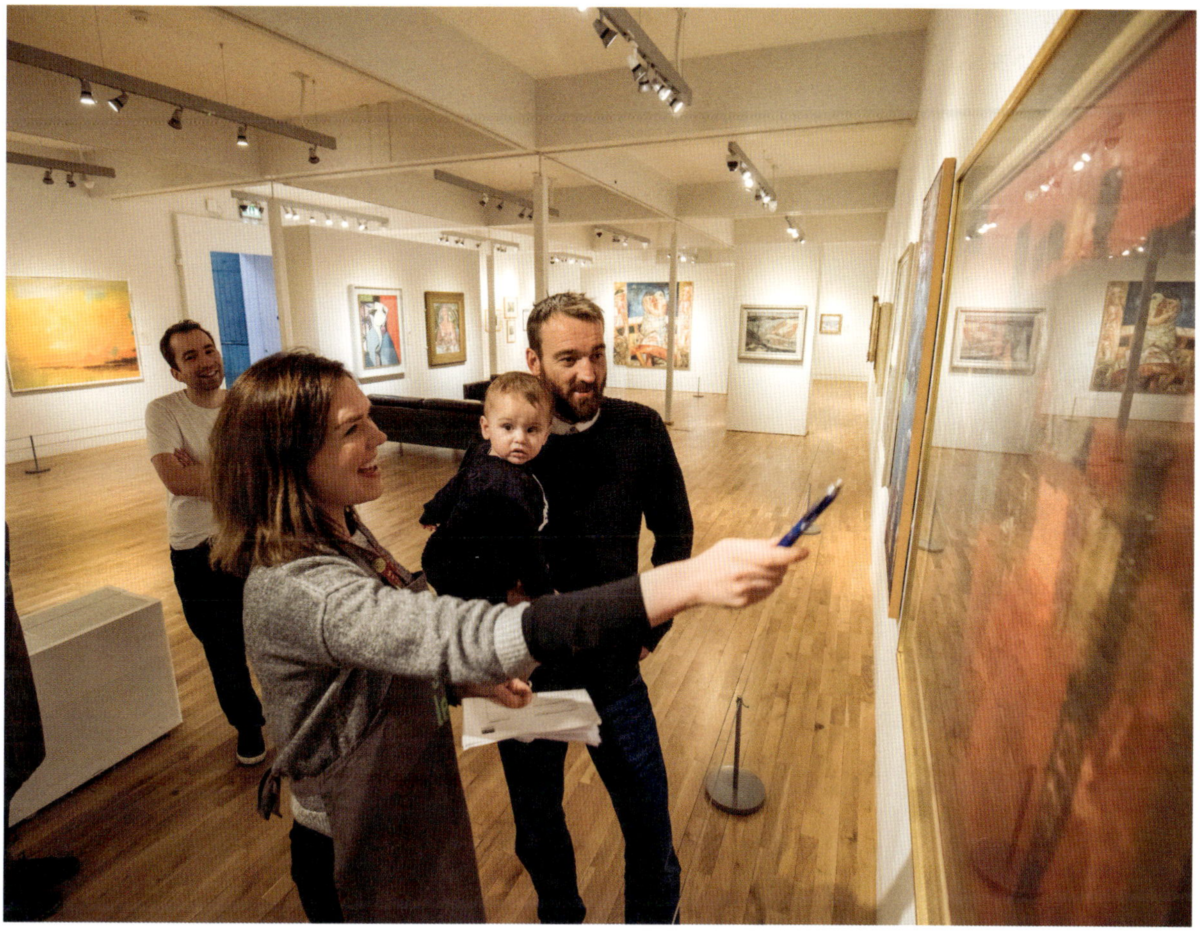

no. 50
Looking and talking about Art with the Creative Learning Team at the *Sense of Place* exhibition

Alan Richardson
Photographer

Alan Richardson started his career in photography while still at school, taking pictures of the drivers and the action at local motorsport events and getting them published in the local paper. Another source of pictures were the star golfers who came to his hometown of Carnoustie to play in the Open Championship. On leaving school he joined a weekly newspaper group based in Arbroath as the darkroom boy and learned the trade by printing the pictures of other photographers. Finally freed from the darkroom he spent the next few years covering everything from car crashes to golden weddings. From Arbroath he moved to Aberdeen Journals working on the Evening Express and Press and Journal where the jobs included Royalty and the famous faces that appeared at His Majesty's Theatre as well as the European Cup winning years of Aberdeen football team. Having won a few awards for his work Alan set up in business for himself in 1989 moving to Dundee where he is still based. His clients include national newspapers, magazines, private companies, academic institutions and public bodies. Work regularly takes him all over Scotland occasionally to London and abroad.

"Choosing a favorite object from the McManus is fraught with difficulty and indecision. Childhood memories, my own children's favorites. I am also lucky to have many personal connections to objects held within its walls, not least a painting of my wife as a child. I am however going to choose the external staircase on the west side of the building, it is one of the most iconic images of Dundee. Photographed every day by tourists, its a meeting place, a vantage point, a children's play ground, a natural stage and a place to sit in the sun and watch the world go by. I have also heard it described as an "affy fancy fire escape."

Anna Day
Author

Anna Day grew up in Dundee and has been visiting The McManus for decades. She was a newspaper journalist on various National papers before coming back to her home town and starting the Dundee Literary Festival. She works on cultural projects across Scotland, is a Cultural Project Manager for the University of Dundee, the manager of the UNESCO City of Design designation and is keenly interested in making the city a brilliant place to live and work. She lives in Dundee with her partner and two daughters, who love the McManus just as much as she does.

"My favourite item in the museum is The Tay Bridge from my Studio Window by James Mackintosh Patrick. I walk past his old house, where he painted this, every day and I imagine him sitting, painting at the window each time."